*A RING OF MAGIC ISLANDS*

# A RING OF MAGIC ISLANDS

*Sybil and Stephen Leek*

**AMPHOTO**
American Photographic Book Publishing Co., Inc.
Garden City, New York

*To Julian Leek, with many thanks for his haunting images of Stonehenge*

COPYRIGHT © 1976 BY SYBIL LEEK AND STEPHEN B. LEEK

Published in Garden City, New York, by American Photographic Book Publishing Co., Inc. All rights reserved. No part of this book may be reproduced in any form whatsoever without the written permission of the publisher.

LIBRARY OF CONGRESS CATALOG NUMBER: 75-27831
ISBN: 0-8174-0587-9

MANUFACTURED IN THE UNITED STATES OF AMERICA

# CONTENTS

| | | |
|---|---|---|
| One | The Immortal Druids | 7 |
| Two | The Isle of Man | 21 |
| Three | St. Patrick's Isle | 35 |
| Four | Primitive Standing Stones | 39 |
| Five | The Isle of Anglesey | 49 |
| Six | Caldy Isle | 53 |
| Seven | Lundy Isle | 65 |
| Eight | Iona the Beautiful | 71 |
| Nine | Islay | 77 |
| Ten | The Isle of Arran | 81 |
| Eleven | Benbecula | 89 |
| Twelve | St. Kilda | 95 |
| Thirteen | Boreray | 101 |
| Fourteen | Callanish Standing Stones: The Isle of Lewis | 103 |
| Fifteen | The Orkneys | 109 |
| Sixteen | Lerwick: The Festival of Up-Helly-Aa | 117 |
| Seventeen | The Isle of Wight | 127 |
| Eighteen | The Channel Isles | 137 |
| Nineteen | The Scilly Isles | 145 |

# One

## The Immortal Druids

When we think of the British Isles, we see two small land masses—one consisting of England, Wales, and Scotland, and the other to the west of these, which is Ireland. The British Isles are steeped in a special antiquity out of all proportion to their size and geographical position. In comparison to the United States, with all its vast resources, the British Isles look like Lilliputians. Yet these tiny islands have withstood constant invasion from early barbaric hordes, as well as from the superior military forces of the Roman legions. True, the Romans landed there in 55 B.C. and made a contribution of good, straight roads and numerous camps, but their cultural influence was much less than one would expect.

The great Spanish Armada, the pride of King Philip II of Spain, was thought to be invincible when it set out to invade England in 1588. When the fleet was off the Isle of Wight, literally a stone's throw from the coast of England, a shift of wind seemed to offer them the chance for an immediate victory. But the wind shifted again and sent the fleet back to Calais. There, British ships sailed alongside the huge Spanish flagships and set fire to them. When a second attempt to invade Britain was made, the Spanish fleet was again repulsed by a change in wind. Thus, Britain was saved from invasion, but this defeat also

Long before Christianity became an established religion, the Celtic Druids performed their religious rites according to the seasons of the year. Although in the past the cult was dominated by males under the leadership of the Arch-Druid, today women hold responsible positions, with no restrictions because of their sex.

marked the final failure of King Philip II of Spain to establish the Church of Rome in Britain. Perhaps there were more than the elements of the universe holding back the invasion of the sacred islands. It is more than likely that the same psychic forces that helped to thwart an invasion by the Germans three hundred years later were already at work.

World War I brought more sophisticated means of warfare to Britain, and again she withstood invasion—only to find herself involved in another war a quarter of a century later. World War II, with its use of planes, rendered the British Isles vulnerable to the superior strength of German war planes and the devastating impact of their guided missiles, unaffectionately called "doodle-bugs" by the populace. The threat of invasion, of alien forces occupying one's native land, is something Americans today cannot completely understand. Such a threat produces a unique type of heroic action, and perhaps one of the most fantastic feats was performed during World War II by a group of followers of the Old Religion, commonly known as witches, but more properly known as Wiccans.

In the New Forest of England, on the south coast of Britain, a group of witches in the Horsa coven decided to produce a "cone of power" as a deterrent to the very near threat of invasion. This is a force created by a group of people with one determined mind, dedicated to performing a single magical action. The thirteen witches gathered, each knowing that every ounce of her psychic power must go into the cone of power. Every witch knew too that her own life was at stake, for the raising of a cone of power can debilitate the life force. Two members of the coven died after the day-and-night concentration, but the cone of power seemed to have worked because the bodies of a small German invasion corps were found in the waters of the English Channel.

The British Isles have always defied great political powers when they felt it was necessary. They have never counted the cost to themselves, even though logically the islands should have been swallowed up by other nations. But the Isles have repeatedly survived against circumstances and odds that not even a dedicated gambler would take up.

The military forces, although superbly trained, have never been numerically superior to other military powers, but the inhabitants of the British Isles possess an inner strength forged from the steel core of tradition. They are closely bound to their homeland through an unbroken link with psychic forces going back to the time of the Druids.

The growth of these psychic forces in the British Isles can best be equated to the construction of a wheel. Like the hub of the wheel, ancient Britain

10

was originally the center of psychic activity in the British Isles. Historic references distinguished it as a refuge for spirits and the home of dramatic examples of the supernatural at work. But through the migration of spiritual leaders—the spokes of the wheel—the psychic forces radiated outward to the wheel's rim—the circle of islands surrounding Britain and Ireland. These are the sacred islands of the west, the home of ancient mystical cults, replete with mysterious occult powers equalled only by those of ancient Egypt. As the spiritual leaders and migration forces settled, the islands became substations of occult power. Just as the human body has a protective aura around it, so the great psychic forces in the islands formed a marvelous aura of protection around the two major land masses. Seen in this light, the survival of the British Isles against alien forces no longer seems surprising.

We owe the beginning of this psychic cloak to the long tradition of Druidism in Britain. The early Druids of Gaul regarded Britain as the womb of their cult, and like all religions, looked with reverence and veneration on the place of origin. The earliest reference to religion in Britain speaks of this mysterious cult. As early as 200 B.C., Sotion of Alexandria referred to Druidism in the twenty-third book of his *Succession of Philosophers*. The question of who the Druids were proved a challenge to theologians and archaeologists for nearly five hundred years.

Druidism probably had its grass roots as far back as the Stone Age, arising out of a cult for the dead. It is a mistake to associate this cult entirely with Egypt. The Druids themselves claimed descent from a god who appears to correspond with Dis, the Latin form of Pluto or Hades. Dis was the monarch of the shadowy region of death who demanded the sacrifice of black bulls. The Druids also worshipped such universal esoteric deities as Mercury, Apollo, Mars, Jupiter, and Minerva.

The Druidic order was a brotherly body divided into three suborders: the bards, who became known as the heroic historical poets; the Vates, or faids, who were the sacred musicians and prophets; and the group of people who were

Huge wickerwork images, such as this Wicker Colossus, were made by the ancient Druids, who filled them with human beings doomed to be sacrificed by fire. Such human sacrifices were generally chosen from among the malefactors of the community, so a crude type of justice was achieved at the same time as the Druidic gods were appeased.

concerned with priestly duties. The brotherhood was ruled over by one supreme leader, the Arch-Druid. It is a mistake, however, to think of Druids only in the context of masculinity. There were also three divisions for women: those who vowed perpetual virginity and lived in sisterhood communities; the married women, who lived with Druids and helped them with their offices; and the concubines, who performed more or less servile tasks.

An elaborate system of philosophy and theology is ascribed to the Druids by ancient schools of writers. The Druids had two sets of religious doctrines: the exoteric one for the community, and the esoteric one for the initiates to the order. In the esoteric doctrine, the Druids postulated a triad of three deities with whom they could communicate; beyond this was a more infinite triad, and above all was a final deity. These seven deities were regarded as stages of divinity, or emanations, very much like the Hebrew Sephiroth. Through each stage, the Druids could communicate with the supreme emanation, their ultimate goal to perfect an alliance with the godhead. The supreme deity was called Hessusm, a name signifying omnipresence. The deity was sometimes called Teutares, a name composed from the words "Due tatt," meaning God the father or creator.

The Druids are often referred to as "teachers of wisdom, who knew the size and shape of the world and the movement of the heavens and stars." They were teachers of a specific way of life designed to help man to know his rightful place in the universe. Their philosophy was based on a consciousness of the environment and metaphysics and an awareness of all elemental forces. The course of instruction to become a Druidic priest lasted twenty years; once trained for the priesthood, many students would go out to smaller communities and in turn impart instruction. The first temples were clearings in woodland areas. These became sacred through the regular performance of rituals within them. Later, circles of stones marked out the sacred areas, and gradually more recognizable stone structures were erected. The most famous of these is Stonehenge, in Wiltshire, England, where a sophisticated form of astronomy and astrology was practiced as part of the religious ritual.

The Druidic alphabet, known as the Ogham script, is believed to have originated in Ireland and South Wales. In this form of writing, letters are represented by groups of parallel lines crossing or meeting a straight baseline. The script was found to be well suited for carving on wood or on stone, the angles of which were often used to achieve the desired effects.

# DRUIDIC ALPHABET

| | | | | | |
|---|---|---|---|---|---|
| ᚱ | B | Boibel | | B | Beith |
| | L | Loch | | L | Luis |
| | F | Foran | | N | Nuin |
| | S | Salia | | F | Fearan |
| | N | Neaigadon | | S | Suil |
| | D | Daibhoith | | D | Duir |
| | T | Teilmon | | T | Tinne |
| | C | Cagi | | C | Coll |
| | M | Moiria | | M | Muin |
| | G | Gath | | G | Gort |
| | P | | | P | Poth |
| | R | Ruibe | | R | Ruis |
| | A | Acab | | A | Ailim |
| | O | Ose | | O | On |
| | U | Ura | | U | Ux |
| | E | Esu | | E | Eactha |
| | J | Jaichim | | J | Jodha |

1st Col.: Bobileth alphabet
2nd Col.: Beth-luis-non alphabet

14

In their search for wisdom, the Druids had to be concerned with every facet of life and death. Thus, while the Druidic cult is well known for its philosophy of learning to live, the old concern with the cult for the dead is also apparent. The Druids were aware that man is not merely flesh and blood, but that his intangible spirit is just as important as the material part of himself. There was, therefore, a belief in the transmigration of the spirit, whereby the spirit survived the death of the body as a force of energy. Through ritual and magical practices, this source of energy could be tuned in to by the living and used to their advantage.

Skeptics have sought to degrade the Druids as mere medicine men with some knowledge of herbs and tree lore; others have seen them as unholy people, lusting for the blood of human sacrifices; and still others have considered the Druids to be superior magicians and sorcerers. The truth is that all of these were different aspects of the Druidic nature, including the participation in human sacrifice, but the Druids were first and foremost the possessors of an enormous storehouse of native learning, which they were prepared to pass on to a specially selected group of initiates.

The ancient Druids ruled their communities with an iron hand and were completely responsible for all civil and legislative matters. On many occasions, two armies at the point of battle would sheathe their swords merely on the intervention of one Druid.

The Druids produced a system of writing based on an alphabet called Ogham, after the Celtic god of learning, Ogmion. Inscriptions in the Ogham script have been found on numerous stones throughout the islands around Britain, as well as on the two main land masses. These stones offer clues to the magical forces that provide the circle of power around Great Britain and Ireland.

By the time Julius Caesar invaded Britain in 55 B.C., there was an already established priesthood of Druidism. Neophytes from all over the world came to these priests, even after the introduction of Christianity. Caesar knew

The Druids also made great use of symbols as a means of communication. The most popular symbol was the circle, associated with the Druidic acceptance of reincarnation as life without end. Other easily recognizable symbols have a link with those used in astrology, a science well understood by the Druids. Here, the symbols for Aries, the south node of the moon, and the horn of Venus can clearly be seen.

about the Druids, probably having derived some knowledge of them from the Aeduan Druid Diviciacus, a friend of Cicero.

> *It is believed that the rule of life was discovered in Britain and to have spread thence to Gaul and today those who would study the subject more accurately journey, as a rule, to Britain to learn it.*
> —De Bello Gallico, *Book VI, 13*

Pliny (A.D. 23-79) is much more specific:

> *At the present time, Britannia is fascinated by magic and performs its rites with so much ceremony that it would seem as though it was she who imparted the cult to the Persians.*
> —Natural History, *XXX, 13*

Druidism was so firmly entrenched in Britain at the time of the Roman invasion that it is difficult to be reconciled to the writings of some historians who indicate that the Romans put an end to the cult. It is more likely that the Druids, through their mysterious powers, were always able to keep one step ahead of any invasion force. Since every known type of divination was observed by the priests, it would be surprising if they did not know when and from where any danger to themselves was likely to come. To know was to be ready for action, even if that action meant a long trek to another place where their religious functions could take place; this accounts for the migrations from time to time to the outer ring of islands. Thus, it would seem that prudence was the better part of valor, that the exile of the Druids from Britain after the Roman occupation was a chosen path taken by the priests, who knew it was more important to carry on with their work than to wait around and be slaughtered by invaders.

Even in those pre-Christian days, the British had great skill as sailors, with ships immeasurably superior in tonnage and sailing capacity to the primitive galleys of the Romans. So it is not hard to visualize the priestly Druids secretly making their way to staunch ships and sailing away from Britain. With their knowledge of the constellations, it was easy for them to make calculations to steer to islands beyond the mainland. On each island, the priests were content to build up their psychic forces, and when they were compelled to leave again and again, these forces remained as vibrations in the ether to be picked up by others who could tune in to them.

It is also probable that the Druids flourished for a long period, masquerading under the disguise of another cult called the Culdee. This cult embraced

Ancient Ireland provided a constant stream of missionary monks who followed the migration route of the Celtic Druids to the tiny islands around Great Britain and Ireland.

a number of Christian monks who resisted and resented Roman authority. Yet their brand of Christianity seems to have been only a veneer covering a doctrine that retained almost all of the old Druidic philosophy. When Augustine arrived in Britain, the Culdees were a strong force. The abbots of the order held office by hereditary right. The monks shaved their heads in the form of a crescent, a relic of the Druidic involvement with the moon as a matriarchal deity. They baptized children by immersion in water, another ritual performed by the Druids, who believed that water was one of the four sacred elements—the others being fire, earth, and air. The Culdees despised the Mass and refused to acknowledge any saints. When condemned as heretics at the Second Council of Chalons in 813, they ceased to function in Britain. Like their Druidic ancestors, they moved to Scotland and finally to the outer islands. Their chief seat under Scottish jurisdiction was the Isle of Iona, the ancient name of which was Innis nan Druidhneah, meaning "the Island of the Druids."

Although the Roman threat to the Druidic-Culdees ended in the fifth century, the cult was aware of the bid from ever-increasing numbers of Christians to take over more and more of the communities. In the sixth century, a post-Druidic priest opposed Saint Columba at Iona. The saint, whose name is now irrevocably linked with the island as a Christian missionary, is said to have had difficulties in building a church there because of magical influences that tore down the walls as fast as they were put up. It is also said that when Columba first arrived in Iona, he was met by a Druid called Boichan and a group of men "disguised in the habit of monks." This seems to add flavor to the idea that the Druids had merged with the Culdees and had made Iona into a sacred sanctuary long before the advent of Columba.

And so on this remote island, two types of magic were to confront each other: that of the Druidic-Culdees, the established mystical cult, and that of Columba, the missionary of a new religion. There was a moral victory for the Cross, but not without some dramatic manifestations of Druidic magic. There are many stories of how the Druidic-Culdees healed the sick, carried live coals without harming themselves, rendered themselves invisible or shifted in shape, made the ice cold water of the river become hot simply by standing in it, and controlled the elements—raising storms at will and walking through them unscathed. Columba counteracted such magic with simple prayers, but diplomatically stated, "Christ is my Druid," thereby acknowledging the existence of the occult religion, long thought to be extinct.

Gradually, as much through the force of numbers as anything else, the spiritual power started by the Druids passed to the more saintly elements of the Christian faith. Columba built up his own legends, which in themselves were not without magical connotations, but his work was ascribed to the new Christian God, not the Supreme Being of the Druids. Stories were told in which Columba's ministers became endowed with the same magical powers as the pagan Druids. Ministers levitated, were clairvoyant, possessed the gift of prophecy, cursed the ungodly, gave utterances while in a trance-like condition, and exercised the gift of healing. In time, these missionaries followed the migration route of the Druids to the circle of islands around Britain and Ireland, often building churches on or near places once held sacred by the early cult.

While the missionaries were pious in attributing their powers to Jesus Christ, the Son of God, members of the community to whom they preached were not partisan in their appreciation. They needed the influence of magic and for many years were not unduly concerned whether the magical powers came from pagan Druids, Celtic saints, old crones, witches, or ministers of the new church. Personal survival was the order of the day, and to survive, the crops had to flourish, territory had to be protected, God and the saints had to be appeased.

This finely preserved Celtic cross in the churchyard of the cathedral at Iona is unique in that it shows Druidic symbols as well as Christian ones.

If a group of people under any name could help these things, then the name of the intermediaries did not matter.

Few religions have attained power by annihilating a former religion, and the people we now call pagans were as dedicated to their type of religion as any of the Christian saints. Instead, the new religion generally takes what it requires from the older one. Thus, while we look to the Isle of Iona as the first stronghold of Christianity, the faith could not have survived without the old belief in Druidism, which paved the way for belief in ritualistic magic as the main trend for religious acceptance. In order to sustain itself, the Christian Church related to old, well-established forms of primitive ritual, taking such ceremonial festivals as Easter and Yule and incorporating them into the framework of its own tenets of religion. If we take magic away from any religion, or if we analyze any down to the bare bones, we have nothing; and man cannot live without a belief in something greater than himself. Consider how much less powerful and effective the Roman Catholic Church would be without the magic of transubstantiation within it, or how much less attractive and understandable the Bible would be without the magic of the numerous miracles mentioned therein. To understand and appreciate Christianity, we have to believe in the miracle of rebirth as manifested in Christ's Resurrection from the dead on Easter Sunday, the day the ancient pagan Druids associated with the rebirth of the earth itself.

Today, the sacred groves and mystical circles of the Druids have given way to vast monuments called churches or cathedrals. Groves, stone circles, and churches are all sacred places where religious ritual and cones of spiritual power have been generated. Such places always retain high vibrations of mystical power, which are passed on from generation to generation. If we accept that there is a special aura within the precincts of a church, we must also accept that there is a surge of psychic forces around the sacred groves and stones of the pre-Christian religion.

Anyone who visits the circle of tiny islands around Great Britain becomes conscious of strong spiritual forces. Just as the planet Earth is protected from the destructive forces of radiation by the Van Allen belt, so Great Britain is protected from annihilation by the steady building up over the ages of psychic forces, created by the Druids and sustained by Christianity.

A ring of magic islands, an unbroken circle of occultism; within this band of psychic power remains tangible evidence of early inhabitants who possessed ancient wisdom. The knowledge is still there for us to tune in and contribute to by trying to understand the magic within ourselves—our most valid link with the godhead of all wisdom, the Supreme Being.

# Two

## The Isle of Man

The history of any country is generally accepted as dating from the time when written records first appear. Before this time, there is always an epoch during which the place is described in sagas handed down by word of mouth from family to family. An unfailing characteristic of such sagas is the stories of those personages who are accepted as founders of a country and ancestors of a race. So in the Isle of Man, we have the famous magician and navigator Manannan Mac Lir as the major figure in folklore. It is not surprising, however, to find Manannan also linked with the history of Ireland, for this country was intimately associated with the Isle of Man until the coming of the Norsemen.

The early Irish legends contain the first mention in history of the Isle of Man, telling us that it was a "fairyland" to which Irish gods and heroes occasionally went to rest. We know that the ancient Druids took refuge on numerous small islands around Great Britain, where they attracted many people who were anxious to learn their ways of wisdom. It is therefore likely that the Irish heroes went to Man to partake of this knowledge.

Of all the Irish deities, the most important to the Isle of Man is Manannan. In order to understand his place in the history of the island, we must

By the tenth century, the people of the Isle of Man no longer regarded the legendary Manannan Mac Lir as an Irish god but as a superman gifted with exceptional powers. In his new role, he became famous for his knowledge of the weather and the treacherous waters around the Calf of Man.

bear in mind that there were five conquests of Ireland itself. The first was by Parthol or Batholoemew, the second by Nemed, the third by Firbolg, the fourth by the Tuatha De Danann, and the fifth by the Milesians. Manannan is connected with the Tuatha De Danann, who were famous for their magical practices. The succeeding Milesians held them in respect, regarding them as members of a spirit world, which ultimately became associated with fairy-lore. There is little doubt that the Tuatha De Danann represent the Olympian gods of the ancient Irish, the hierarchy of divine beings that became the heritage of the Celts. In this hierarchy, Manannan was saluted as the god of the sea.

By the tenth century, however, this belief in Manannan as an immortal deity was modified to a glorification of his unusual powers as a mortal man. It is thus that we find him described in the *Glossary of Cormac*, the early Irish literature written by the King-Bishop of Cashel who died in A.D. 903:

*Manannan Mac Lir, a celebrated merchant, was in the Isle of Man. He was the best pilot that was in the west of Europe. He used to know by studying the heavens, the period which would be fine weather and the bad weather, and when each of these two times would change.*

In this manner, the legendary idea of weather magic evolved for which Man is still famous.

To Cormac's account, the historian E. Donovan added:

*Manannan was the son of Allot, one of the Tuatha De Danann chieftains. He was otherwise called Orbsen, then Loch Orbsen, now Lough Corrib. He is still vividly remembered in the mountainous district of Derry and Donegal (in Ireland) and is said to have an enchanted castle in Lough Foyle. According to the traditions of the Isle of Man and the Eastern counties of Leinster, this first man of Man rolled on* three legs like a wheel *through the mist.*

The "three legs of Man" has since become the main motif of the island.

According to the Book of Femoy, a manuscript of the fourteenth century, Manannan "was a pagan, a law-giver among the Tuatha De Danann and a necromancer possessed of power to envelop himself and others in a mist so he could not be seen by enemies." Again we find a link with the Druids through their reputation of being able to make themselves invisible and change shape at will in order to confuse and foil their enemies.

Still another manuscript speaks of Manannan in his mortal guise:

*The merchant Orbsen was remarkable for carrying on a commercial intercourse between Ireland and Britain. He was commonly called Manannan on account of his intercourse with the Isle of Man, and Mac Lir, meaning "he who springs from the sea," derived from the fact that he was an expert diver; besides, he understood the dangerous parts of the harbors and from his prescience of the change of weather, always avoided the tempests.*

The association of Manannan with the Isle of Man probably arose in this way. It was the practice of the earliest Irish to represent their divinities as living on islands to which, under exceptional circumstances, mortals might sail. Because of the close proximity of Man, and with Manannan's love of the sea, it is natural that he should have spent more and more time on the isle. When the Milesians began to overthrow the Tuatha De Danann, Manannan retired to the Isle of Man. Legend has it that Manannan kept the isle covered with a mist, and tales were told in which he was seen as a giant. One sage said that Manannan could transport himself with ease across the gorge between Peel Castle and Contrary Head. His grave is said to be the green mound, thirty yards long, outside the walls of Peel Castle, and now called the Giant's Grave.

Manannan was attributed with all the characteristics that go with the image of a superman, and perhaps to be a superman, any man must first know the glory of being a god and then relate it to life as a human being. Manannan could move huge rocks and wield a large sword, become invisible, and make his enemies see him as a hundred other persons. Most of all, the tradition of magic hung gracefully on him, and to this day, the Manx people—descendants of the great and mighty Manannan—have the reputation of being magicians.

Saint Patrick went to the Isle of Man, but first he sent a convert there named Mac Cuill. Mac Cuill sailed over in a coracle, a fragile boat made of hide stretched over a wicker frame. When he reached Man, he found two men waiting for him. It is said that they welcomed him from the sea and that he learned the divine rule from them. Mac Cuill, who later became identified as Maughold, ultimately founded a bishopric and was eventually made a saint of the Christian faith. On the Isle of Man, a church was dedicated to Maughold, and many healing miracles are attributed to him.

The fairy-lore of the Isle of Man is only rivaled by the legendary leprechauns of Ireland. The Manx conception of a fairy seems much the same as in other Celtic lands. They are supposed to be like human beings in face and feature, and they love to live in green hills and woodlands. They are partly human and partly spiritual in their nature. Some are benevolent, curing men of disease and aiding them in misfortune; others are mischievous and quick to avenge themselves on humans for any variety of reasons. They enjoy attention, and on Midsummer's Eve, many island dwellers put out offerings of flowers and herbs

Among the numerous unique achievements of Manannan was his ability to roll on three legs like a wheel. The "three legs of Man" thus became the national emblem of the island.

25

for the little folk. On the same night, they hold a fairy court and in their revels leave behind rings in the grass.

Fairy Hill, near Rushen Castle, is supposed to be the domain of the King of the Fairies. In folklore, the fairies were supposed to be the original inhabitants of the Isle of Man, and everything on the island was carried on in a supernatural manner. They maintained a blue mist over the island so that no sailors would know they were there. The mist was sustained by a perpetual fire, but one day it was allowed to go out and the Isle of Man was revealed to mankind. The land of the fairies was then invaded by a race of giants, presumably the Tuatha De Danann, of whom Manannan was the leader. The fairies, however, safely entrenched themselves on the site of Rushen Castle, where they remain to this day for those to see them who have the gift of second sight or who are "fey."

In Rushen Castle, there is an apartment which, in the memory of living man, has never been opened. The native Manx people say there is "enchantment in this apartment." They will tell you that the castle is the home of fairies, and that it became the home of giants who continued in possession of it until the days of Merlin. This mighty sorcerer, by a feat of magic, dislodged most of the giants but bound the rest of them by spells until the end of the world.

A Manxman will tell the story of some men of more than ordinary courage who ventured to explore the subterranean apartments but never returned to give an account of what they saw or found. Even today, Rushen Castle remains famous for its subterranean passages. There are some psychics who believe that they lead to an underground city inhabited by giants, but any attempt to explore the area is always aborted.

The Isle of Man is also famous for its own version of the popular children's story called "Jack the Giant Killer." Once upon a time, there was a poor woman who lived in a secluded glen on the eastern side of Slieuu-ny-Farrane. Her husband was a fisherman who was away for long periods of time, so the woman had to manage her children on her own. One boy, Jack, was always getting into trouble and would fight anything and anyone. He grew large in stature and earned the nickname of Jack the Giant Killer. His strength was so notorious that many men came from Laxey to try their strength against him, but Jack was always the victor. Wild boars roamed through Duidale, one of which was known to be very ferocious. Jack was determined to kill this boar, so he went in search of him. He found the boar luxuriating in the water at Crummag and went in with a big stick to tackle him. The conflict was a bloody one; Jack was badly wounded but he managed to kill the boar. Jack crawled home, but weak from loss of blood and badly wounded in the leg, he was forced to use a crutch for the rest of his life. So the neighborhood got rid of two terrors: the boar, who was dead, and Jack, who was rendered harmless. So the association with giants and magic persists in the tiny Isle of Man.

In addition to the magic of the Druids, Manannan, Saint Patrick, and the fairies, there was also a famous prophetess called Caillagh-nyp Ghueshag, who belonged to a coven of witches. Besides the ability to prophesy, she could transport herself miraculously to distant places and gained quite a reputation for healing. But as with most people who have this gift, she could also inflict many hurts on those who displeased her. She used the Evil Eye on them so that they withered in body and died. On the whole, her powers were used for good rather than evil, and this tradition of witches as charmers, well versed in the use of herbs, is still sustained today.

By Statute 33, Henry VIII declared all witchcraft and sorcery to be felonies. The ultimate penalty was death. The Isle of Man also legislated on this subject:

> *All such as are suspected of sorcerie and witchcraft are to be presented to the Chapter Quest, then the Ordinary, in such cases finding any suspicious, is to impannel a jury of honest men within the parish and the party suspected in the meantime to be committed to the Bishop's Prison; and all the offences and crimes the jury doth find the Ordinary shall write, and if the jury can prove any notorious fault or crime done by the same person, then the Ordinary to deliver him out of the Bishop's Prison to Lord's Jail and Court.*

If one court did not get the witches, another would, for the accused were often condemned to be thrown into one of the many green bogs that are plentiful in the Isle of Man. The most famous bog for this purpose was the Curragh Glass, in a valley below Geeba Mountain. If the witch sank, she was considered innocent and given a Christian burial, but if she swam ashore, then she was guilty and could be sentenced to any one of several unspeakable means of elimination. The seventeenth-century manuscripts in the archives on the Isle of Man are full of such cases of witchcraft.

The history of Man, like that of many other places, is replete with stories of how Christians came to the isle and lived side by side for many centuries with those who followed the old nature and folk religion of witchcraft, which should more properly be called Wicca, meaning "the craft of the wise." We find

Legend has it that beneath the strong fortress of Rushen Castle remains an even more impregnable subterranean stronghold, home of a race of giants who were also powerful magicians.

evidence of this in many customs that are still practiced today.

Both the Celts and Norsemen, before the introduction of Christianity, held festivities at the beginning of summer and winter, the midwinter and midsummer festivities being more especially of Scandinavian origin. As Saint Patrick and his missionaries gained converts to Christianity, they were confronted by a populace demanding that these feasts should still be held. So the celebrations were wisely incorporated into the folklore and continues to be semi-pagan to the present day. Such ancient observances as perambulating the land boundaries became Christianized and associated with divine worship. The sources of water, made into wells, were dedicated to saints and martyrs of the church. After the Reformation, the practices of visiting these holy wells and of frequenting the tops of mountains at Lammas—the harvest festival of August—were denounced as wicked, but no amount of theological disapproval succeeded in wiping them out.

January 1, New Year's Day, was formerly called "Little Christmas Day" and was the occasion for feasting and festivity. No one worked on this day. To meet a cat was considered unlucky, and part of the festivity included the ritual of choosing a lucky person to set the "first foot" in all households. This is an old Celtic custom which today we associate mainly with Scotland, but which is still in force on the Isle of Man.

Twelfth Night was also celebrated long before Christianity spread to the isle. On this day, no one could borrow fire from anyone else but had to purchase it. On the Isle of Man, it was a day when all the inhabitants danced; in olden times, the dance involved cavorting around a fire. Many games were devised for this day, including the one known as Goggans, or Noggins. The Noggins, which were small mugs, were filled with symbols of trade, such as water for a sailor, meal for a farmer, and the like. The Noggins were laid in front of the hearth by the men; then while the girls were out of the room, the order was changed around. The girls came back blindfolded and each picked a Noggin. According to what was in it, the girl could so expect to find out the trade of her lover and expect to marry him within a year.

January 25 is now commonly called the Feast Day of Saint Paul, commemorating the conversion of the saint to Christianity, but to the ancient Manxman, it was the day when he could divine the weather for the year. If the day were windy, then the year would produce famine and many deaths would occur. If the day dawned bright and fair, there would be an abundance of corn and other crops.

Shrove Tuesday seems to have been observed in the Isle of Man in much the same way as in England. It was the custom to eat a dish called sollaghan,

A serene and spiritual place, the Monks' Bridge in Ballasalla was well known to the early monks who came to the island.

made of oatmeal and gravy. This was consumed for breakfast, followed by meat and pancakes for dinner. But the Manxmen warned against having a full stomach in case one should know the pangs of hunger after Easter.

Saint Patrick's Day, March 17, was a day of activity when seeds were sown, but a relic of the old witchcraft cult remained, as salt was also put into the ground to purify it against evil influences.

On Easter Sunday, the ancient Manx people would go to the top of the nearest mountain. There are many versions of sun worship that stem from this, even though it became an official Christian festival.

On May Day Eve, the fairies were not forgotten; green boughs and flowers were offered at each doorstep. To keep away evil from the field, handfuls of gorse were burnt. Kelly, in his *Manx Dictionary*, refers to the use of fire thus:

> *The inhabitants kindle fires on the summit of the highest hills, in continuation of the practice of the Druids, who made the cattle and probably the children pass through the fire, using certain ceremonies to expiate the sins of the people.*

Since fire played an important part in Druidic festivals, it is no wonder that Saint Patrick tried to prevent the Manx people from making their yearly trek to the mountaintops and observing the old festivals of fire. But the ancient Manx placed great reliance on the influence of fire to protect them from evil. This is probably a throwback to the legend of the fairies who kept fires going to cause the blue mist to rise over the isle and keep it safe from invaders. The Norsemen also held festivals of fire, so by the time Saint Patrick came to the Isle of Man, the habit of using fire as part of festivities was well established.

May Day, or Beltaine, was one of the great Celtic feasts, marking the beginning of summer. Cormac, in his *Glossary*, says that the name Beltaine arose "from two fires which the Druids of Erinn used to make with great incantations." The name Beltaine in Gaelic means "Bel's fire," "Bel" being the name of the sun in this language and "tein, tine, or taine" signifying fire.

The festivities of Midsummer's Eve were introduced by the Norsemen, for the Celts did not place any special importance on the longest day of the year. However, to dwellers in the north, a day when the sun made its lengthy appearance was obviously an occasion for festivity. This festivity was in honor of Balder, the northern god of the sun who at Midsummer attained his greatest splendor and from thence began to decline. Manxmen celebrated Midsummer's Eve with bonfires on the hilltops; blazing wheels were rolled down the hillside and again cattle and young children were driven between two fires to purify them and keep them safe from illness and disease.

In ancient times, both October 31 and November 11 were celebrated as Samhain Eve, the proper occasion for prophecies to be made. Again the fairies had to be propitiated by leaving food and fresh water for them. Samhain festivities are the opposite in character to those held in May, for now the sun is in its decline and the forces of darkness can take over. Bonfires were lit, however, and various rituals to the sun were observed.

On December 24, the mummers, consisting of groups of dancers and fiddlers, went from house to house. In Man, the mummers were called "The White Boys," and they would enact the time-honored legend of St. George and the Dragon. The houses chosen to be visited would be immune from any evil forces attacking the occupants in the coming year.

The church festival of Christmas was observed at the same time as a pagan feast of the winter solstice. The Romans called it Saturnalia and the Norsemen called it Yule, but whatever the name or the reason for the feast, Christmas Day remains a time for festivity—of eating, drinking, and making noise, either by song or by music. The pagan festival of Yule lasted until January 6. The Christian Church attempted to change these festivities, believing that so much merrymaking was not in keeping with the solemnity befitting the birth of Jesus Christ. The result was that in the Isle of Man, a strange medley of both Christian and pagan rites contributed to the festivities of the modern Christmas.

On December 26, what now seems to be a most cruel festivity took place. On this day, boys would catch a wren and carry it on top of a pole from house to house. At each stopping place, a feather was pulled from the little bird until it was naked. Then it was buried with great solemnity and serious ceremony, followed by wrestling and all manner of sports. The sacrifice of the wren was supposed to be in memory of the first Christian martyr. Yet here again we have a link with the Druids, for they called the wren "the king of birds" and showed great respect for it. As a sign that Christianity was supreme over Druidism, the wren was chosen to represent death of the ancient cult. But in the Isle of Man and other Celtic islands, the wren is still called the druai-eean, or "Druid's bird." It is an interesting point to note that England continued to revere the wren, and it is still considered unlucky to kill this bird or rob its nest of eggs. Instead of the legend of the wren, however, England provided its own version of bird-killing in the legend of Cock Robin.

The early religious structure in the Isle of Man was always linked with a reverence for the phenomena of nature, especially the elements, once again

Born without a tail and with striking markings, the Manx cat is unique. Its ancestry is still an enigma, although short-tailed cats are found in parts of Russia, Japan, China, Siam, and Malay. With its distinctive personality, the Manx cat seems much more likely to be the "familiar spirit" than the proverbial black cat associated with witches.

indicating that the Druidic cult did not give way easily to the missionary work of Saint Patrick. Of all the phenomena, nothing was so sacred as the sun, which was benevolent, yet mysterious and awesome. The connection between the sun and man-made fires is an intimate relic of sun worship. The moon and the stars, as mitigators of darkness, were also recipients of adoration, but to a lesser degree. It is highly probable that the belief in charms against fairies and witches was encouraged by the early teachers of Christianity as a means of diverting the minds of their converts from their worship of nature and nature spirits, personified by animals and trees. In the Isle of Man, there is also an unusual superstition about letting any blood fall on the earth. When William Christian was shot at Hango Hill in 1662, a blanket was spread on the ground so that not one drop of his blood should defile the earth. Since blood was involved in the sacrifices of the Druids, it is not likely that anything so mystical should have been wasted.

On no other island in the world have the dual rituals of Druids and Christians been so well maintained as on the Isle of Man. Christianity slowly took over from the practices of the Druids and the sun rituals of the Norsemen, but the people of Man are well known for their resistance to changes of any kind. Many of their proverbs indicate that a cautious man is a wise one, and the Manx people are solidly careful "ta aile meeley jannoo bry millish." This means "a slow fire makes sweet malt," but also translates as "don't be in a hurry," "don't jump to a conclusion."

The inhabitants today are a mixture of Celtic romanticism and Scandinavian practicality, and no one is going to wrench their fairy-lore from them until there is something better to put in its place. The increase of intercourse with England and Scotland, the large emigration of the Manx and the immigration of strangers, and the shoals of visitors who frequent the island in the summer with the consequent increase of wealth and prosperity have produced natural results. But beyond the well-trodden tracks of tourists, there are still places away from town and highways where belief in fairies, hobgoblins, witches, and ghosts still remains.

Here in the Isle of Man, modern witchcraft has retained its hold. People still visit the island to consult a witch or someone who can cast an Evil Eye. Even the legendary familiar of witches, the cat, is different on Man, for there is a breed of tailless cat indigenous to the island.

The Isle of Man is still the home of mystical magic, where the psychic forces vibrate as the spirit of old Manannan causes the mist to shroud the island in a protective cloak. It has always made its own terms with the rest of the world, and there seems no indication that it will change.

# Three

## St. Patrick's Isle

This tiny island is situated on the west side of the river Neb on the Isle of Man. St. Patrick's Isle is connected to the mainland by a causeway linking it to Peel, one of the major seaports of the Isle of Man.

It is here that Saint Patrick founded the first Christian church on Man. There is a small chapel dedicated to the saint, which dates back to the eighth century. There is also the ruined cathedral of Saint Germain, which must have been very impressive in the tenth century, complete with its bishops' palace. It is always amazing to realize that the early Christian missionaries never thought any island was too small for them to erect a church or cathedral upon. Having followed the Druids, they were probably aware that wherever the Druids set up their teaching communities, there would be enough people to appreciate a church.

Dominating the isle are the ruins of Peel Castle, immortalized by Sir Walter Scott in his romantic novel *Peveril of the Peak*, and a round tower reminiscent of the ones found in Ireland. Also on the isle is a large artificial mound of even greater antiquity than Peel Castle. Another mound, outside the walls of the castle, is known as the Giant's Grave, which is believed to contain the remains of Manannan Mac Lir, hero of the Isle of Man.

(Above) St. Patrick's Isle is actually part of the Isle of Man, but Irish monks who visited there chose to build the first Christian church on the tiny isle rather than on the main part of the island. (Right) The ruins of Peel Castle, close to the remains of the early cathedral, indicate that despite its size, St. Patrick's Isle was once an important spiritual and secular area.

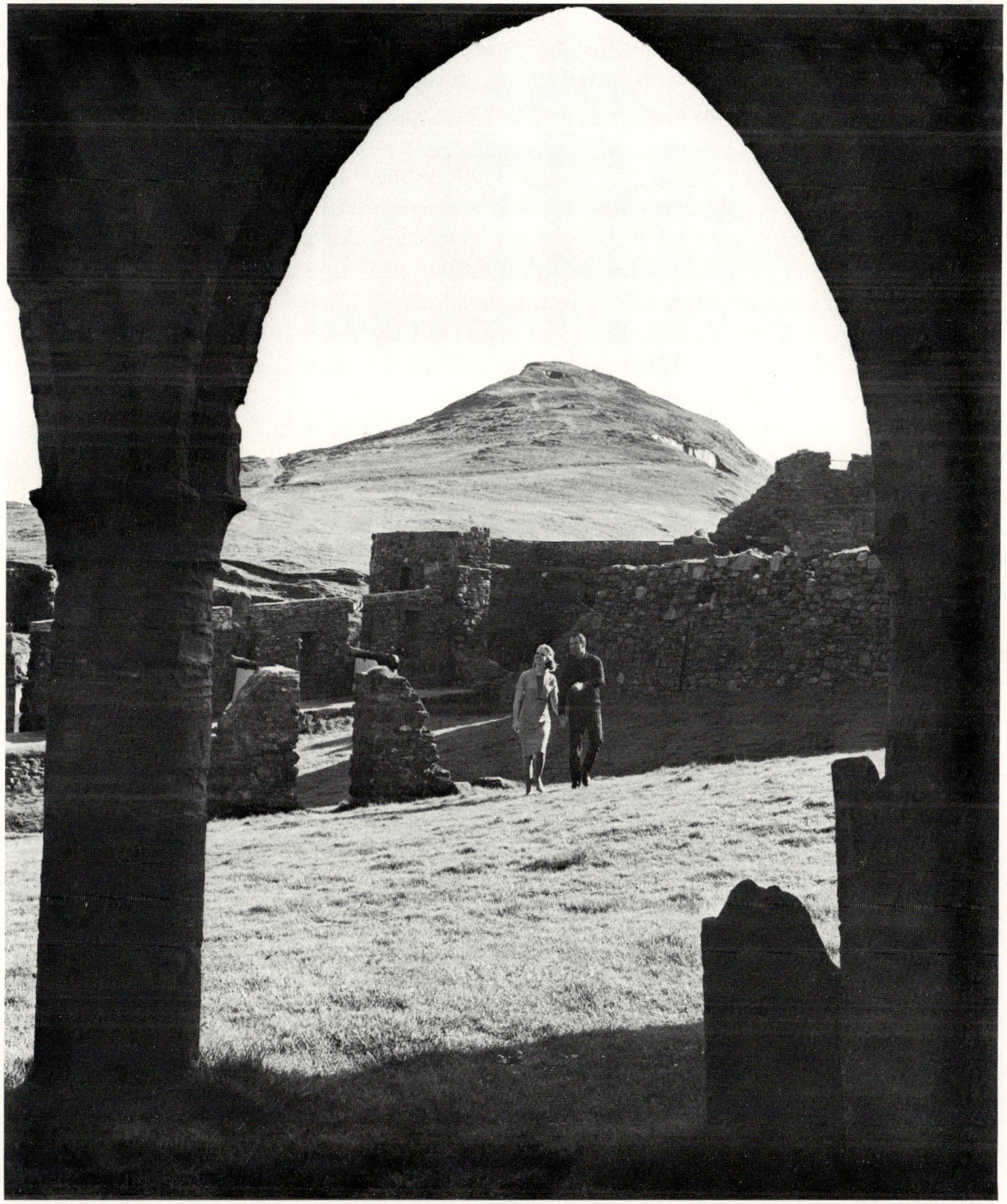

St. Patrick's Isle, often shrouded in a mysterious mist, is an excellent place to visit, especially for those people with psychic awareness. It is not difficult to see the ghosts of departed spirits, as well as the materialized vision of Moddey Dhoo, the great black dog mentioned in Scott's novel, who is said to roam around the Giant's Grave.

The legend of the dog is interesting. Through one of the old chapels in Peel Castle, there was formerly a passage to the apartment belonging to the Captain of the Guard, but it is now closed up. An apparition, called the Mauthe Doo in the Manx language, frequently appeared in the shape of a large spaniel with shaggy, curly hair. He wandered at will around the castle, but as soon as the candles were lit, he would come and lay down by the fire in the presence of the soldiers. Although they became used to it, no one cared to be left alone with the ghostly dog.

It was the custom for one of the soldiers to lock the gates of the castle at a certain hour, then carry the key to the Captain of the Guard. No single man was courageous enough to do this duty, so two men always attended to it. One night, a soldier got very drunk and said he was not afraid of the dog, even if it were the devil in disguise. His fellow soldiers tried to dissuade him from going to lock the gates himself, but he went anyway. The soldiers heard a great noise and the drunken soldier returned, literally looking as if he had seen the devil. For three days and nights he did not speak, although his companions begged him to tell them what had happened. He died a horrible death, with face and body distorted. That night, in 1666, the great black dog did not come when the candles were lit, but from time to time he is still seen roaming around Peel Castle.

# Four

## Primitive Standing Stones

As much history has been bequeathed to us through stone monuments as by the written word. The raising of stone monuments is a practice that can be traced to many countries. Stone has an obvious advantage over other natural materials in that it allows monuments to defy the elements as well as the destructive hands of men. Our ancestors who erected stone monuments did so with specific purposes in mind, high motivation, and probably the desire to leave a message for future mankind.

Stone monuments fall into several classifications. Isolated pillars of unhewn stone are called monoliths, or menhirs. Sometimes they are found arranged in a straight line, forming an avenue that leads to another circle of stones. If their linear arrangement forms a circular or oval enclosure, the group is called a cromlech. When monoliths are placed closely together to enclose an area sufficiently small and narrow enough to be roofed over by one or more stones, they form a chamber known as a dolmen. In rare instances where a dolmen is made up of two single standing stones supporting a third one overhead, like the lintel of a door, the monument is called a trilithon. A superb example of trilithons can be seen at Stonehenge, in Wiltshire, England.

All the existing standing stones in the world today were originally set up for specific purposes. Single monoliths generally commemorate the burial places

40

of kings and chiefs or mark the site of a battle. Others define boundaries of land used for religious and sacred purposes. Although standing stones are primarily associated with pagan man and his rites, Christians also erected them in groups of twelve and seven. Wherever Druids made their home, they erected stones to delineate sacred pieces of land, such as those at Stonehenge and at Callanish, off the east coast of Scotland. With the introduction of Christianity, it was not unusual for missionaries to make use of existing menhirs to support a cross or the figure of a saint.

On White Island, in Fermanagh, Ireland, there are eight well-preserved examples of carved monolithic figures. Made in the eighth century, they were originally part of the monastic building at Castle Archdale Bay, in Lower Lough Erne, although they are now housed in a derelict church. It is thought that when the figures were moved to the Christian church, they were placed in a secluded spot because their pagan origins and design became embarrassing. Two of the monoliths represent bishop-like figures complete with croziers, one portrays a warrior, and another depicts an erotic female figure called a Sheila-na-gig. The monoliths range from two to four feet in height, and each has a socket at the top of the head. These sockets were probably used to hold sacred fire or water for ceremonial purposes.

Another example of a carved monolith can be found on Boa Island, in Fermanagh. This double-headed figure, with a head on each side of the monolith, represents Janus, the God with Two Heads. Although Janus was known to the early Celts, who gave him the status of a deity, he was also one of the major Roman gods. Regarded as the origin of all things, he represented the male and female principles of life, as well as the polarity of night and day. With his two heads, he could gaze into the past or look into the future. He was also the god of doorways because a doorway serves the dual purpose of being an entrance or an exit. There are many explanations about the function of Janus, and monoliths of him were once in great favor because he had the power to protect households, temples, sacred land, and the exit from life to death.

The Ring of Broghar, an intriguing circle of monoliths, is a fine example of primitive standing stones.

In the center of the circle, the small trilithon is reminiscent of the enormous one at Stonehenge.

Heaps of stone piled up in a conical form are called cairns. In ancient times, they were erected as sepulchral monuments, marking the resting place of a chieftain or spiritual leader. This neolithic cairn at Glenvoiden, on the Isle of Bute, is one of several on the coastline.

(Above) These carved monolithic figures on White Island, in Fermanagh, Ireland, are pagan in origin but were moved to a Christian church in Ireland, where their pre-Christian significance proved to be an embarrassment to the clergy. The head of each figure is scooped out to form a socket; it is quite likely that sacred fires were burnt in the head of each effigy, which in turn leads to the premise that they were once part of a ritual temple. (Right) The two-faced figure of Janus, on Boa Island, is associated with Roman mythology. The name is generally explained as being the masculine form of Jana, also known as Diana, the goddess of the moon and mistress of the hunt. Janus was regarded as the beginning of all things. As such, it is appropriate that January, the first month of the year, is named after him. The ninth day of the month was once celebrated as a festival in his honor. Janus is also associated with the pre-Christian religion of Wicca, commonly called witchcraft, which has links with Druidism. Since Ireland was once a stronghold of Druidism, it is interesting to note that Janus was also worshipped as the god of the oak tree—the sacred tree of the Druidic groves. The Janus of Boa Island may well have been the stone guardian of such a grove, where it kept watch on the opening into the grove.

45

(Above) When a monolith has a hole in it, such as the Holestone of Kilbridge-Doagh has, it indicates that it was used as part of fertility rites. Male and female would pledge themselves and then clasp hands through the hole. This "hand-fasting" ceremony is becoming very popular today with modern covens of witches. (Right) The capstone of the Legananny Dolmen of Dromara is over ten feet long; the stones mark a burial ground nearly a thousand feet above sea level.

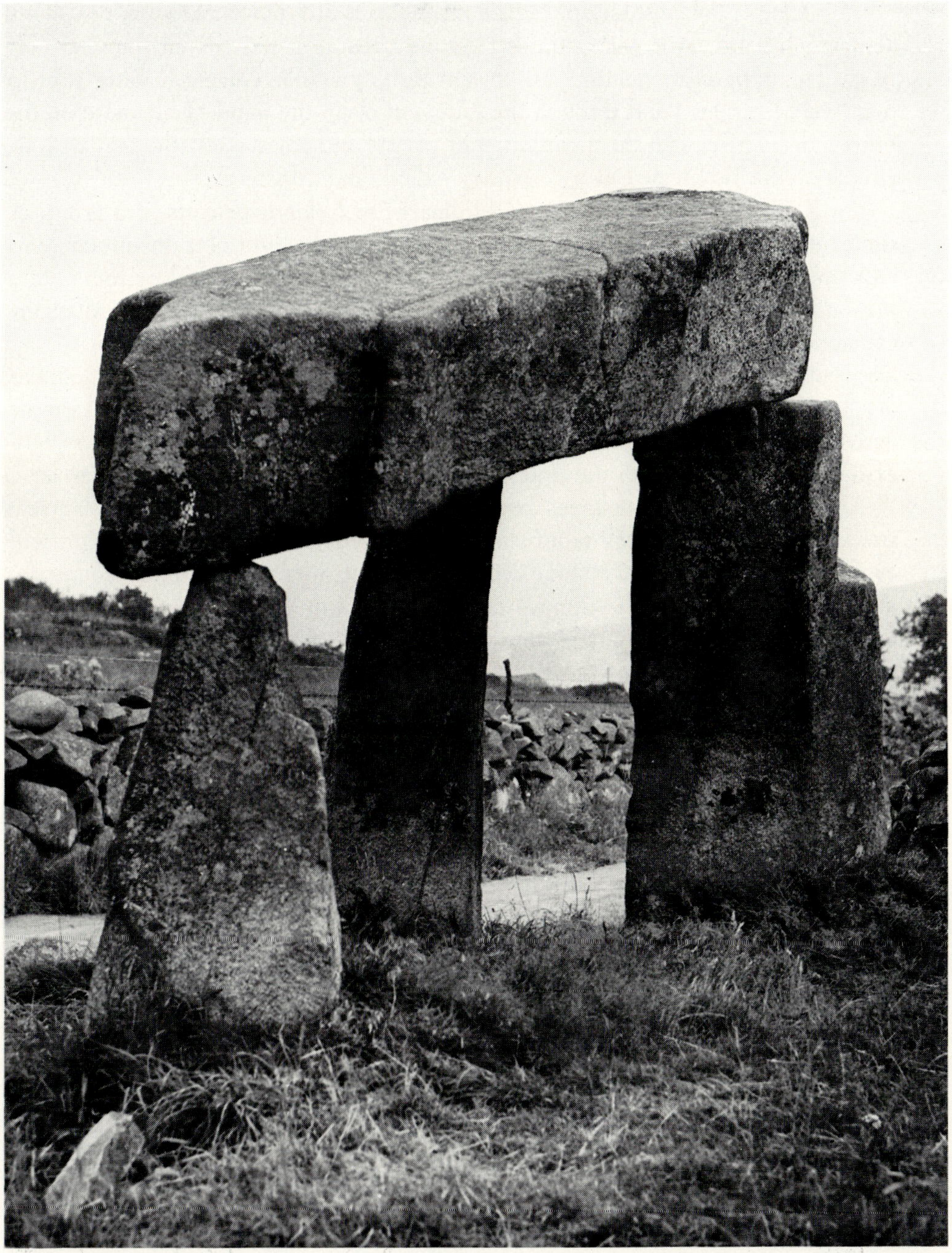

One of the most unusual single monoliths is at Kilbride-Doagh, in County Antrim, Ireland. It is called the Holestone because it has a well-rounded hole in it. This type of monolith is an ancient fertility stone. During fertility rites, a man would put his hand through the hole and clasp the hand of his mate on the other side. Then, with the incantation of priests and priestesses, the union of the couple would be blessed in a ceremony called "hand-fasting."

The Legananny Dolmen of Dromara, in Ireland, consists of a group of stones impressively placed some thousand feet up the side of a mountain, and was probably erected to mark the burial place of an Arch-Druid or some other person of great importance in the community. The uppermost stone, called the capstone, is over ten feet long in this dolmen. Dolmens of this size are more frequently found in Europe, so its size makes it unique in the Isles. Small dolmens are located on the Isles of Anglesey and Man, both bailiwicks for Druidic activities. Generally, if one looks around the vicinity of a dolmen, one can find evidence of a circle, with the dolmen serving as the entrance to such a circle.

Monoliths and dolmens remain our most tangible link with the ancient wisdom of the past. There is no chronological sequence in the construction and evolution of these primitive stone monuments, but they exist in many countries, always being linked with religious ceremonies—both pagan and Christian. To our ancestors, they were just as important as the massive cathedrals and churches that evolved with the growth of the Christian religion.

# Five

## The Isle of Anglesey

The ancient name for Anglesey was Mona. Situated off the coast of Wales, the isle is separated from the mainland by the Menai Straits, made famous in 1826 when Telford constructed his controversial suspension bridge linking the mainland to the historic island.

In early times, Anglesey was a refuge for the Druids who refused to stay in England under Roman rule. Suetonius Paulinus, the first Roman Governor of Britain, attacked the island in A.D. 61, only to be confronted by a horde of wild-eyed women. The Roman historian Tacitus refers to the noise made by the Druids when Paulinus was about to attack their sanctuary on Anglesey. Holding torches and shrilly screaming like the Furies, the women rushed into the center of the Roman legions. Meanwhile, the Druidic priests surrounded the invading forces. Weaponless and with hands held high up toward the heavens, the priests chanted invocations, which the Romans interpreted as curses. At first this unexpected onslaught repelled the Romans, until urged on by their generals, they systematically slaughtered most of the women and many of the priests.

Paulinus then commanded that every tree in the sacred Druidic groves be cut down. In these groves, the sacred fires were kept burning. The groves were sometimes circular because the Druids regarded the circle as the emblem

(Above) Din Lligwy, on the Isle of Anglesey, is the site of the massive stone remains of an ancient Celtic house. (Above right) This stone structure is the chambered tomb at Din Lligwy. (Right) The Romans used the emblem of Brazenface, the Celtic god of the sun, in many of their ornamental public baths during their occupation of Britain.

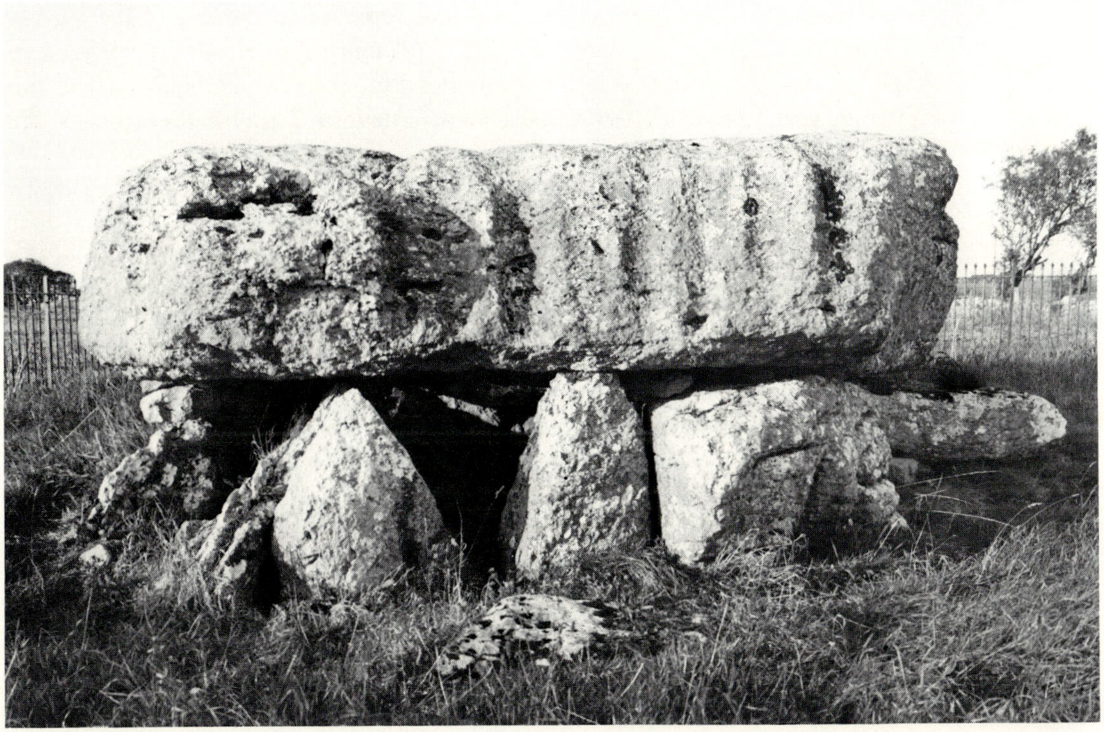

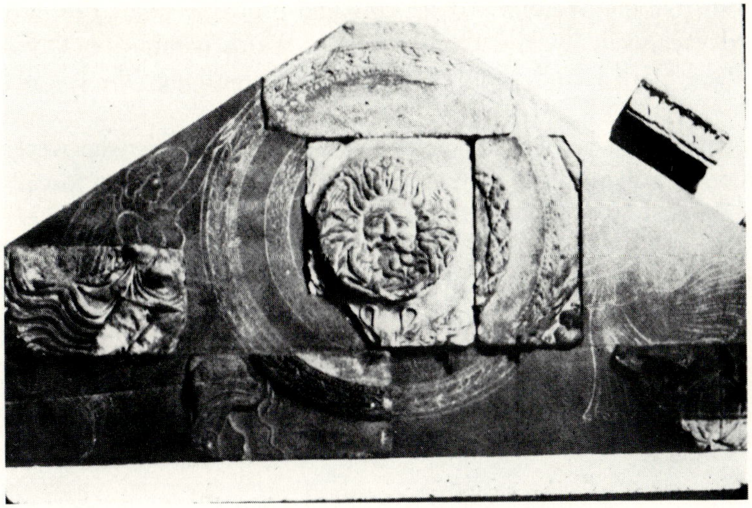

of the universe. Other groves were oval and represented the egg of the world, the symbolic origin of the universe itself. Still more groves were serpentine in shape because the serpent was the symbol of Hu, the Druidic equivalent of the Egyptian god Osiris. A few groves were cruciform because the cross is the symbol of regeneration.

The slaughter of the Druids, followed by the sacrilege of cutting down the groves, seemed like the end of the strong Druidic forces on the island. But as Paulinus set up his own garrison, a number of Druids who had survived the holocaust moved quietly away from Anglesey toward the Isle of Man.

It is interesting to note that Wales, the most accessible part of the mainland to Anglesey, was the country that saw a grand renaissance of Druidism in the twelfth century, a tradition that has remained to the present day. The white bulls kept by the ancient Druids as beasts for sacrifice have also survived in small herds in England and Wales. At St. Teilo, in Wales, there is an Oxen Well, indicating that this part of Wales was under the influence of the Druids of Anglesey. Until 1812, a bullock was always sacrificed when disease broke out in the Welsh herds. It is not unusual to find plaques shaped like a bull's head in settlements known to be under the authority of the Druids. This type of plaque is called Old Brazenface, one of the many titles of the old Celtic god of the sun. Anglesey was one of the principal seats of Druidism, and some twenty-eight cromlechs remain on the island, generally situated on high land overlooking the ocean, such as the one at Plas Newydd.

The Isle of Anglesey is known by many names, the ancient one Mona having been derived from the Welsh word for cow and probably related to the white herds owned exclusively by the Druids. Other Welsh names are Ynys Dywyll, meaning "the Dark Island," and Ynys y cedyrn, meaning "the Isle of brave folk."

Anglesey is indeed a verdant monument to the brave Druids who were prepared to sacrifice their lives rather than submit to rulership by an alien force. Confident in their magical arts, the indestructible Druids lived to colonize other islands for many centuries, leaving behind an aura of sanctity and psychic forces built up around the once sacred groves.

# Six

## Caldy Isle

Caldy is a small island off the coast of Pembrokeshire, on the mainland of Wales. The first Celtic monastery was founded there in the sixth century. Today, there is a thriving community of monks who live and work in a monastery built on the site of the previous one in the thirteenth century. The present monastery area includes the Church of Saint Illtud, named after a knight at the Court of King Arthur.

A link with the early Druidic influence on the island is the Ogham stone, which curiously enough remains inside the Church of Saint Illtud. Stones like this are among the few written relics of Druidic times, but the lettering is often symbolic rather than a straightforward text. This particular stone dates from the sixth century, but it has been Christianized by the addition of the cross above the writing.

The present-day monks are engaged in agriculture, which mainly consists of growing food to support the monastery, but a thriving business has also been built up by growing lavender. From this sweet-smelling herb, a perfume is made, which is sold extensively on the mainland.

For many years, women were barred from Caldy Isle. Now, however, they too are permitted to visit this peaceful haven of spirituality, although they

Caldy is the home of a thriving community of monks who live and work in a monastery there. For these monks, this beautiful island is a version of Shangri-la.

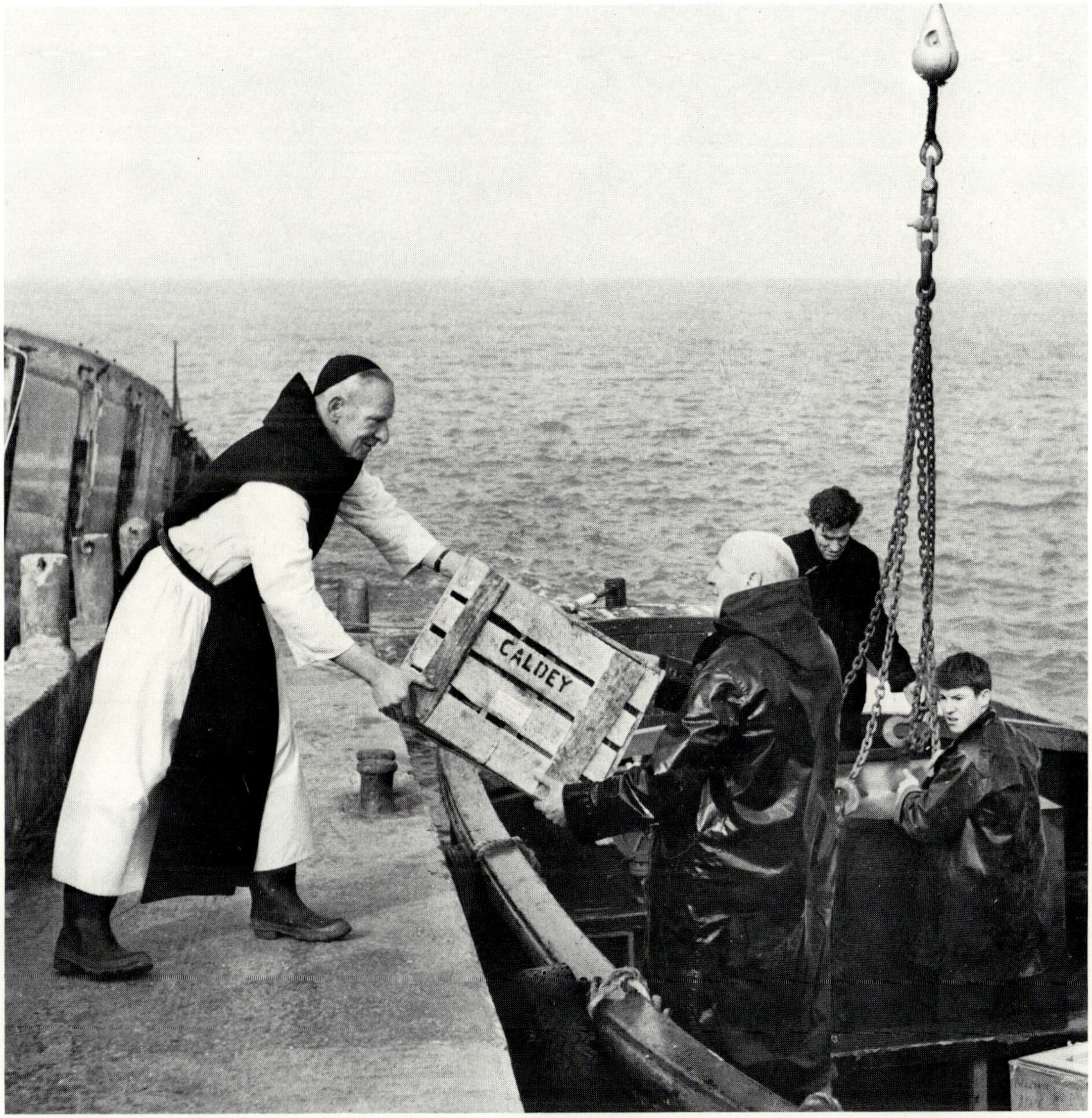
CALDEY

56

(Left) With its Druidic script and Christian cross, the Caldy Ogham stone is a memorial to two great spiritual forces, bridging the past and present, who found sanctuary on this island. (Above) The monks who live in Caldy Abbey take a vow of silence.

The monks of Caldy Isle tend the lavender shrubs from which they manufacture a popular perfume. The sale of this perfume on the mainland provides a source of income for the monastery.

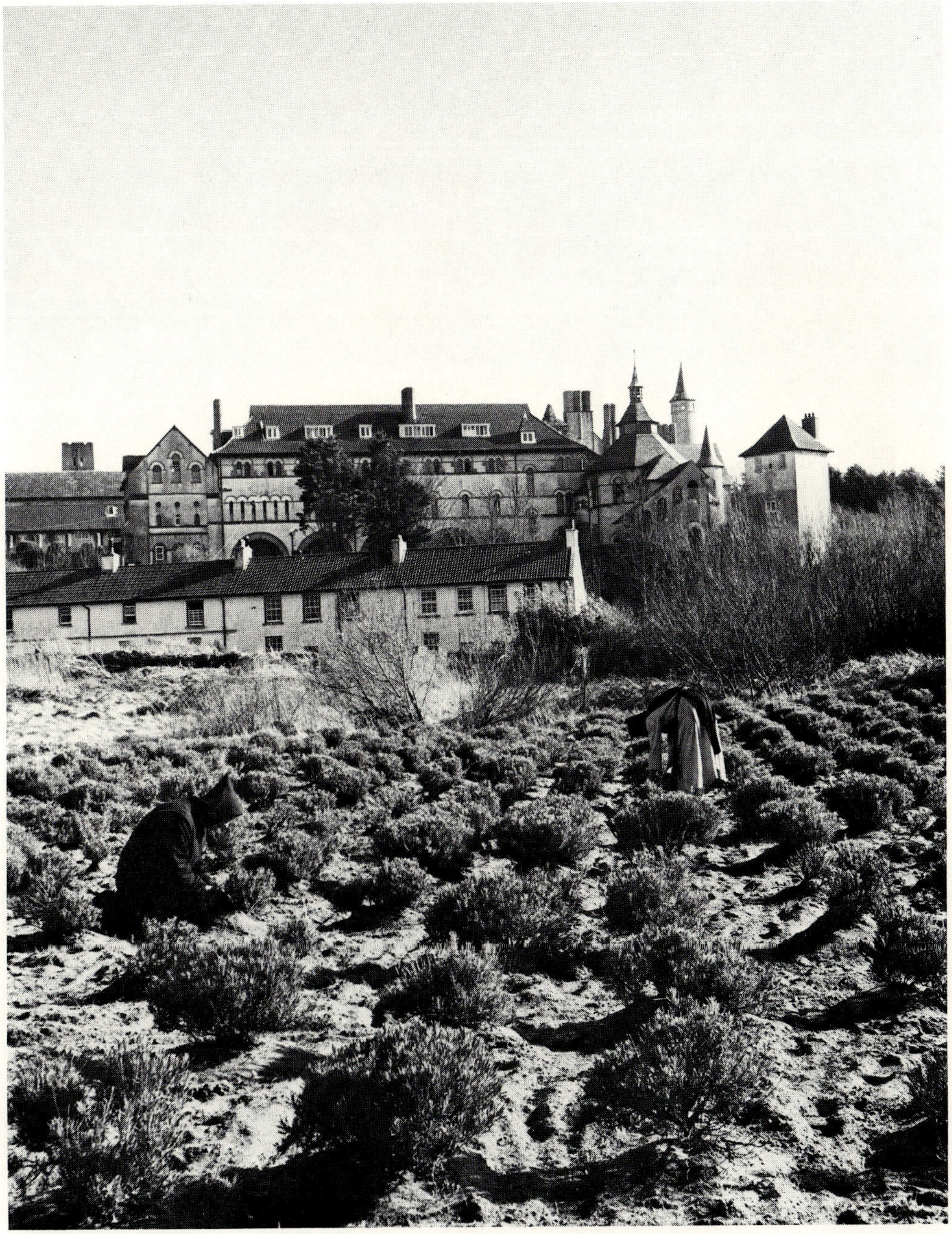

Prayers for the living are a daily obligation of the monks.

The church is dedicated to Saint Illtud, a knight at the Court of King Arthur.

(Above) Cross and cassock stand in mute solitude. (Right) In ancient times, missionary monks lived in the natural rocky caves around the coastline. Peaceful meditation can still be observed in this cave.

63

The waters around the island are deceptively gentle on this day as two monks rest and meditate.

still may not set foot in the monastery. Those people who have visited Caldy speak of the serenity of the area, where great powers of psychic forces have been built up in an unbroken tradition from Druidic times to the present Christian involvement.

When the west wind blows over Caldy, the perfume from the lavender fields wafts over the mainland, but some of the psychic forces drift from the island as well. Men and women alike gaze toward this delightful island from the mainland and feel some of the serenity seeping into their beings.

**STONEHENGE**
    (Above) Although the massive stones at Stonehenge reflect the unique engineering skill of the early inhabitants of Britain who erected them, they also stand as a powerhouse of psychic vibrations. These vibrations radiated outward to the numerous islands surrounding Great Britain, building up a protective aura around England, Scotland, Wales, and Ireland over thousands of years. (Over) The last rays of the dying sun strike the main structure on a cold November evening. Most visitors go to Stonehenge at dawn to watch the rising sun strike the stone altar, but the ancient circle is equally as impressive at sunset.

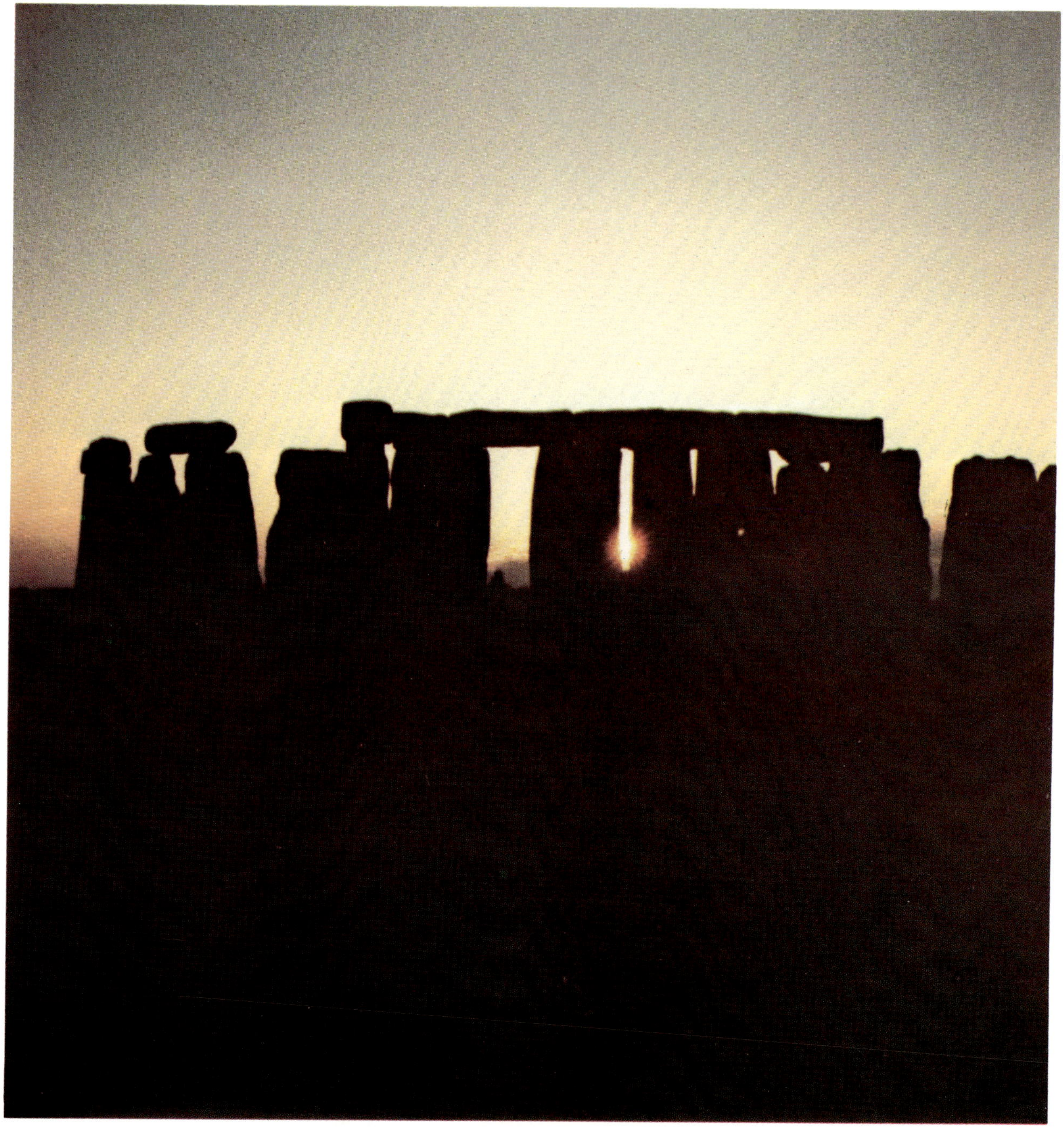

RELICS OF THE PAST
(Above) Since white bulls were kept by the ancient Druids as beasts for sacrifice, it is not unusual to find plaques shaped like a bull's head in settlements known to be under Druidic authority. This type of plaque is called Old Brazenface, one of the many titles of the old Celtic god of the sun. (Right) Inscriptions in the Ogham script have been found on numerous stones throughout the British Isles. These stones offer clues to the magical forces that provide the circle of power around Great Britain and Ireland.

## HOLY ISLAND

(Above) When Saint Aidan came to preach Christianity to the Northumbrians, he chose the island of Lindisfarne as the site of his church and monastery and made it the headquarters of the diocese he founded in 635. (Right) Target of the first Viking raid on England in 793 A.D., the Priory and its grounds are haunted by the ghosts of murdered monks.

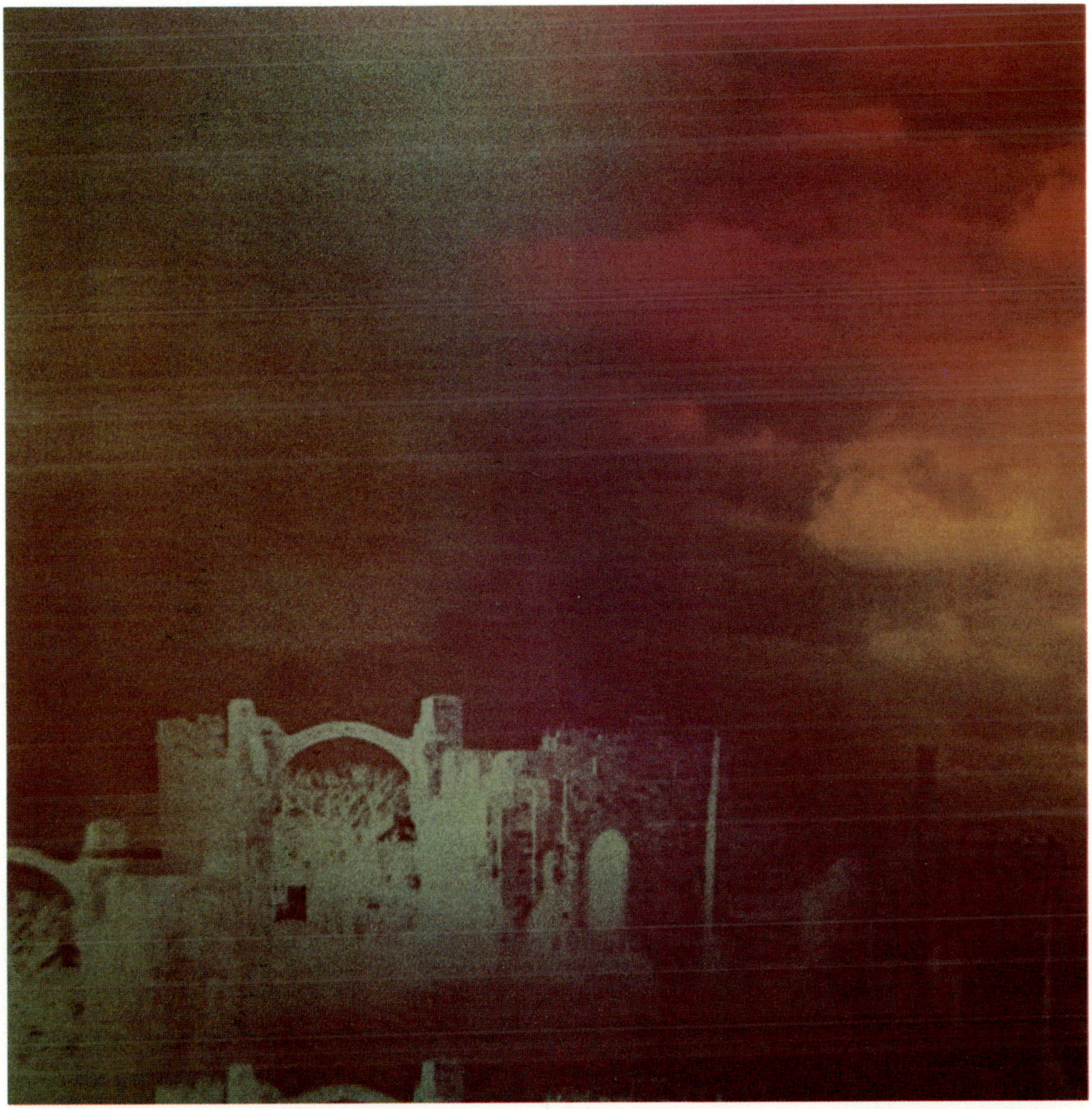

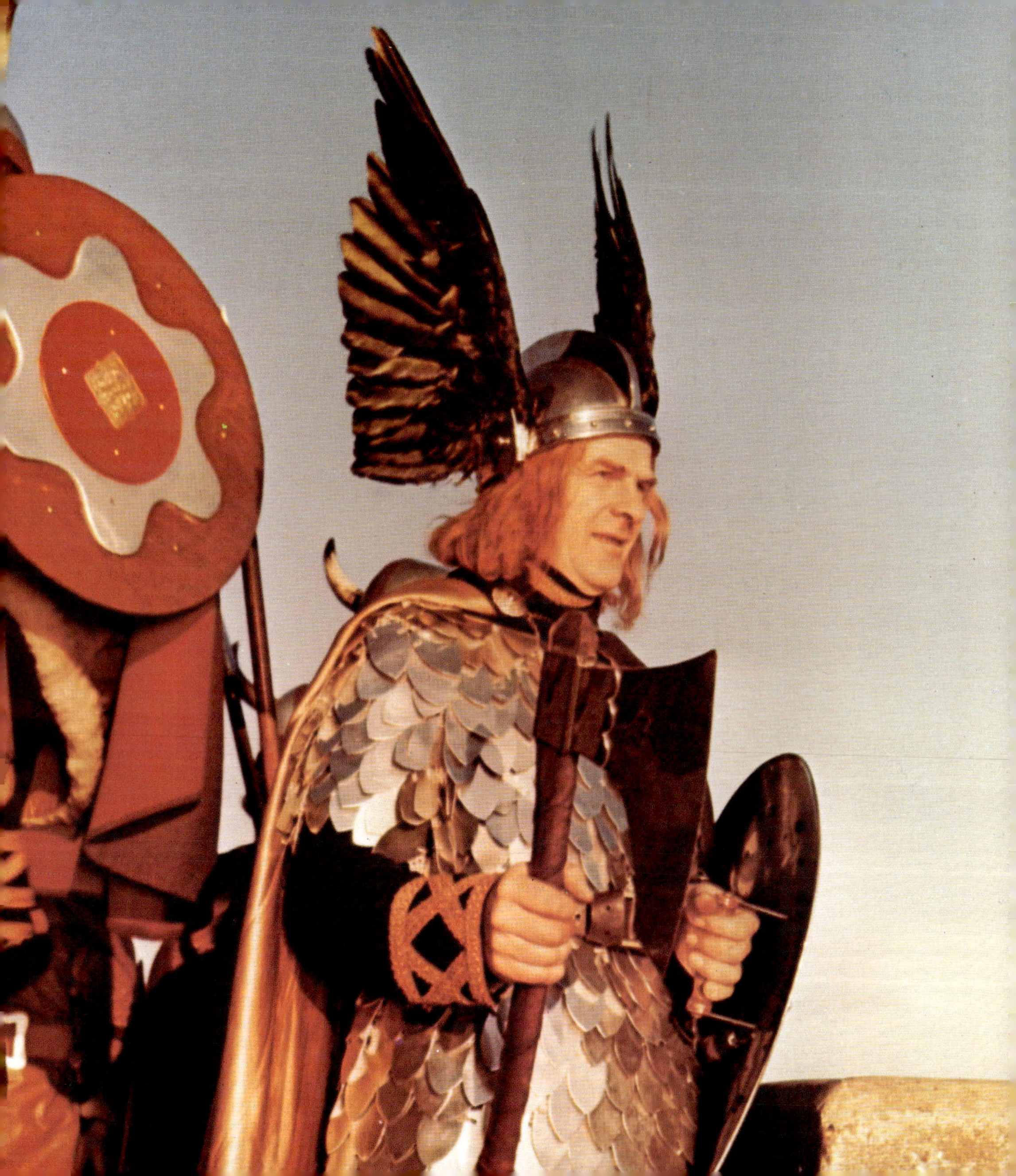

**UP-HELLY-AA!**
　　(Left) A Lerwick islander, resplendent in Viking costume, stands ready for the annual festival of Up-Helly-Aa. (Above) Against the night sky, the sacrifice to the sun-god is a truly remarkable sight.

## FAIRIES

The little folk are part of the folklore of all islands. St. Kilda is steeped in superstition, with fairy-lore providing some of the more attractive stories.

# Seven

## Lundy Isle

Situated at the entrance to the Bristol Channel, Lundy Isle is easily accessible to the coast of Devonshire and the lovely ports of Clovelly and Bideford. Lundy is built on granite, some of which was taken from there to construct the famous Victoria Embankment in London.

Communication between the island and the mainland is now excellent. The journey by plane takes about fifteen minutes, and the crossing by sea three hours. Although a regular service is scheduled, there is always the wayward weather to contend with. This and the rocky, treacherous coastline have given Lundy a unique history of shipwrecks and marine tragedies. To a great extent, Lundy has thrived on the misfortunes of others, but unlike some of the other islands, Lundy has no need to wreck ships deliberately in order to plunder them. Its geographical position can be relied upon to achieve the same results, and most of the families on the island have enjoyed the loot from one shipwreck or another.

In 1813, Lundy was linked in an obscure way to the American War. The second Leeward Island Fleet was homeward bound and had to pass up-channel in one of the thick fogs that suddenly envelop this area in a terrifying, impenetrable shroud. When the fog lifted, the U.S. brig *Argus* found herself in the middle of eleven hostile warships. Action took place, during the course of which the American brig sunk the British *Mariner*. The waters that flow so sweetly at times on the shores of Lundy sing a constant requiem to several hundred men buried in this part of the Atlantic Ocean. The island has all the charm of a beautiful woman who promises so much but in the end turns out to be a femme fatale.

Lundy is a unique place in every way, a maverick that exists on its own guiles and wiles, and there is something about the isle that defies the rest of the world and treats it with an air of disdain. Like the mountain that the avid mountaineer feels compelled to climb because it is there, so Lundy exists to challenge the sophistication of another world on the mainland.

Man has survived on Lundy since 7000 B.C., when it was a camping ground for the nomadic Mesolithic hunting groups. In the Neolithic period, *circa* 3500 B.C., the island was invaded by men from the mainland who worked in stone and brought with them their own powerful magical religion. The Bronze Age, *circa* 2000 B.C., brought more settlers from the south of England, and their custom demanded the building of round burial mounds. There is a burial ground known as Bull's Paradise which dates back to this pre-Christian time and which was probably linked with Druidism, since we know the Druids regarded the bull as a sacred animal.

The history of Lundy is strangely silent from the eighth until the twelfth century, when the Orneyinga Saga of 1148 tells of activity from Viking invaders. At this time, the island was mainly inhabited by members of the De Marisco family. Although originally of Norman heritage, they had strong connections with Wales, and so a link with the Druids must have been maintained then. The De Mariscos were a powerful family who also held estates in the county of Somerset, England, and in Ireland. The family was generally in a state of unrest and consequently had many enemies. Lundy, therefore, was a halfway house for their activities and a place to retreat to when times were bad on the mainland or in Ireland. In Marisco Castle, their inaccessible and beautiful fortress, the De Mariscos lived lawlessly until 1242, when Sir William Marisco was hanged following an unsuccessful attempt to assassinate Henry II, the ruling monarch of England.

When the Black Death scourged the mainland between 1325 and 1335, many ministers found refuge on the island and remained there until Henry VIII, indefatigable and ruthless in his determination to dissolve all monasteries, successfully wrought havoc on those still on Lundy.

Nature provides a rich bounty from the ocean; here, an inhabitant of Lundy Isle brings in the seaweed harvest.

In 1625, the island was attacked by Turks, and in 1633 by Spaniards. After this, it survived to become the main attraction for many groups of French privateers who found it a good place to hide from their enemies.

In the middle of the nineteenth century, the island came under the care of a man appropriately named Mr. Heaven, a jealous guardian of its rights. He became the unofficial, but *de facto*, governor of the island, to which he brought organization and industry. His son, licensed as a curate, held his services in a crude hut in the High Street. The hut later ceased to be used as a primitive church, and it is used today as a place to dip sheep. A legacy from Mrs. Langsworthy, who was born Sarah Heaven, enabled her relations to build a permanent stone church. This building, completed in 1896, was dedicated to Saint Helen. Despite the fact that it is an architectural eyesore, in far-from-tasteful Victorian Gothic style, it is this church which finally gave Christianity a stronghold on Lundy. Christianity had been a seesaw of popularity from the time the Roman authority collapsed. Since Lundy was very accessible from Ireland, the invasion of missionaries helped to Christianize it long before the other islands off the coast of Britain.

Even in 1931, Lundy was still determined to be a maverick. At this time, a Mr. Herman became the owner of the island and decided to issue his own coinage. These Lundy coins, called Puffins and Half-Puffins, after the island's original Icelandic name are collectors' items today. (The puffin is also a favorite bird on the island.) Herman also tried to dismiss any link with the regular mail service and issued his own stamps.

*The Times* of London fully reported the unique case brought by the Attorney General, Sir William Jewett, King's Counsel, against Martin Coles Herman. The Attorney General referred to Lundy as "a sort of Utopia," but the case went against the resourceful Mr. Herman. It proved a hollow victory, however, for Puffin coinage immediately went up in value and the island still issues its own Puffin stamps.

Except for the tiny island of Sark, in the Channel Isles off the coast of France, Lundy is the only British Isle that does not pay any income tax; in fact, the only levy they are required to pay is toward the National Health contribution. Neither do the liquor licensing laws apply on the island, where the Marisco Tavern is open as long as there is a thirsty soul requiring a drink. The mainland police have no authority there, but law and order is the responsibility of the owner of the island. So, in a way, Lundy is still "a sort of Utopia."

Relics of the past remain on the island, the best known site of which is Beacon Hill. Located near the site of Bull's Paradise, Beacon Hill seems to have always attracted attention as a spiritual locale. Here, four early Christian memorial stones carry these inscriptions:

1. Igerni   I Tigerni      5th–6th century
2. Potit                   8th century
3. Optimi                  5th–6th century
4. Resteuta                5th–6th century

It is strange to find so few funeral stones when the island is replete with flat-topped cairns, or "leacht," of much greater antiquity.

The ancient cemetery on Beacon Hill also contains the outline walls of an old chapel dedicated to Saint Elen. It is more likely, however, that this chapel was originally dedicated to Elen, the wife of Mixim Wledig, King of Britain, who died in A.D. 388. There is a record of a secondary foundation, dating back to 1254, which was also dedicated to Saint Elen.

In 1640, a church dedicated to Saint Ann made its appearance, and Saint Ann's Chapel on Beacon Hill continues to be in use. In 1787, another church was built in the Beacon Hill area, this time dedicated to Saint Helen, but it is now in ruins. It is interesting to note how close the Christian churches were always built to those sites once dedicated by the Druids for their own ceremonies.

One of the most awe-inspiring sights on Lundy is the Giant Caves, discovered in 1860. Here, two 8-foot-long skeletons were unearthed with a few artifacts. Archaeologists place the date of the skeletons in the ninth century and believe them to be the remains of Viking chieftains. The bodies were found in a main-chambered tomb with their heads resting on large stone pillows.

Today, Lundy remains something of an enigma, frustrating in its effects on those who visit it. Some see it as one of the most romantic of all the islands, while others shiver at sinister vibrations touching on the macabre. Now leased by the Landmark Trust to the National Trust, it has become a major tourist attraction. The maverick days seem to be over, but Lundy still supplies an aura of magic, which is enough to give wonder and appeal to the jaded palate of a world that has just begun to discover the word "ecology."

We should never forget that the primitive people who found a haven on Lundy were very aware that they had a special place in the universe. They left us another legacy of stones from which we can trace the steps of the Druids and the evolution of Christianity.

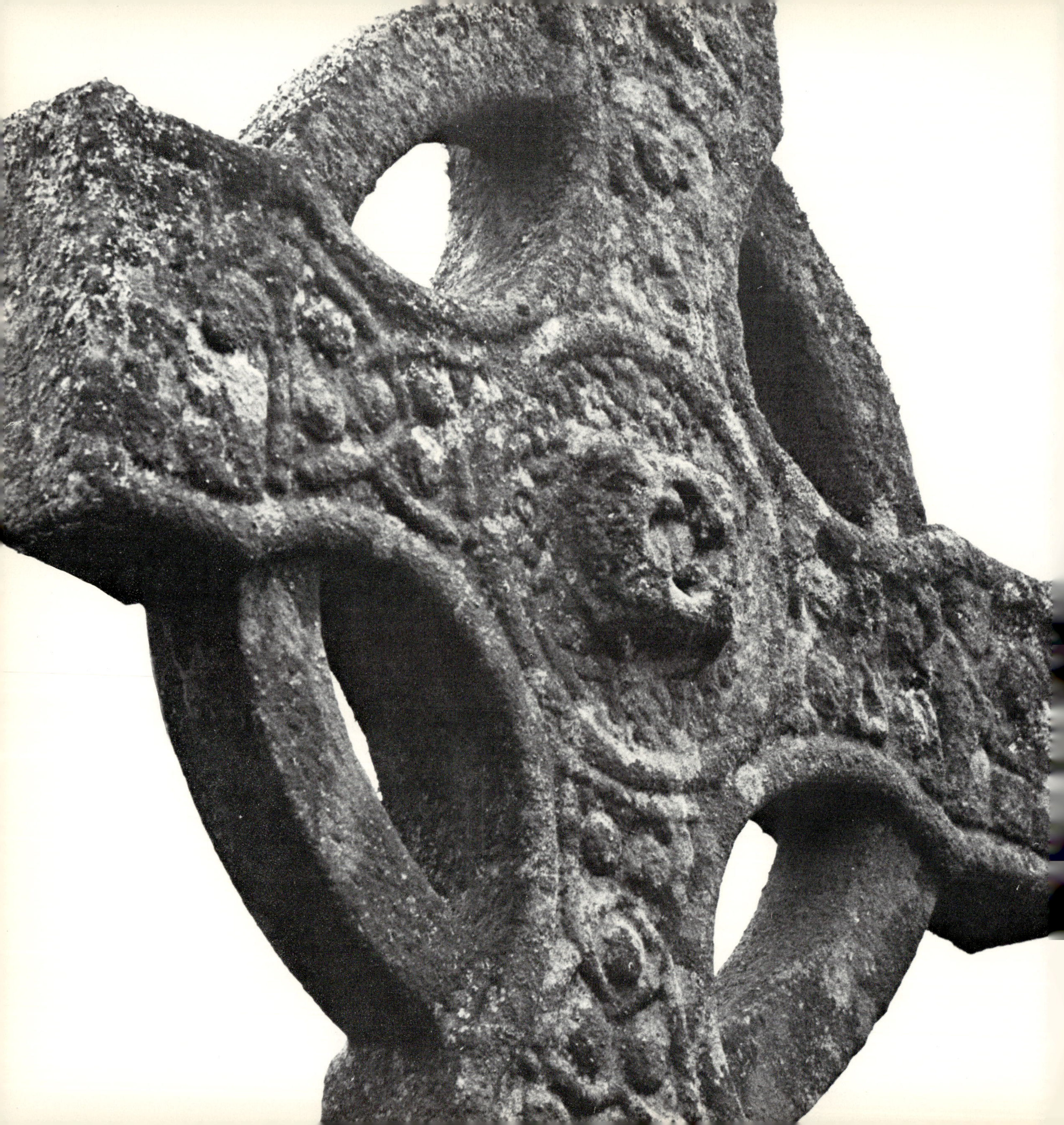

# *Eight*

## *Iona the Beautiful*

Iona is an island of the Inner Hebrides group. Its Druidic name was Innis nan Druidhneah, meaning "the Island of the Druids." When the Christian missionary Columba established his church there in 563, it became known as Icolmkill, that is, "the Island of Columba of the Cell."

Iona is probably one of the most sacred areas in the world, first through the establishment of the Druids, then as the center of Celtic Christianity, when it became the mother community of numerous monastic houses. Students came to Iona to work with Columba, and many missionaries were sent out to spread the gospel on the mainland. At the death of Saint Columba, pilgrims came from far and near to die in this sanctified spot. However, the fame and wealth of the monastery also attracted less welcome visitors. The longboats of the Norsemen began to sack the Hebrides, and Iona was looted.

In 801, the church was burnt down, but many monks survived—only to be caught up in a new holocaust in 806. Eighty monks were put to death at Martyrs' Bay, but others managed to escape and found their way to Kells, in Ireland. They took with them the relics of Saint Columba encased in a gold and silver shrine. The population of monks, however, was tremendous, and there

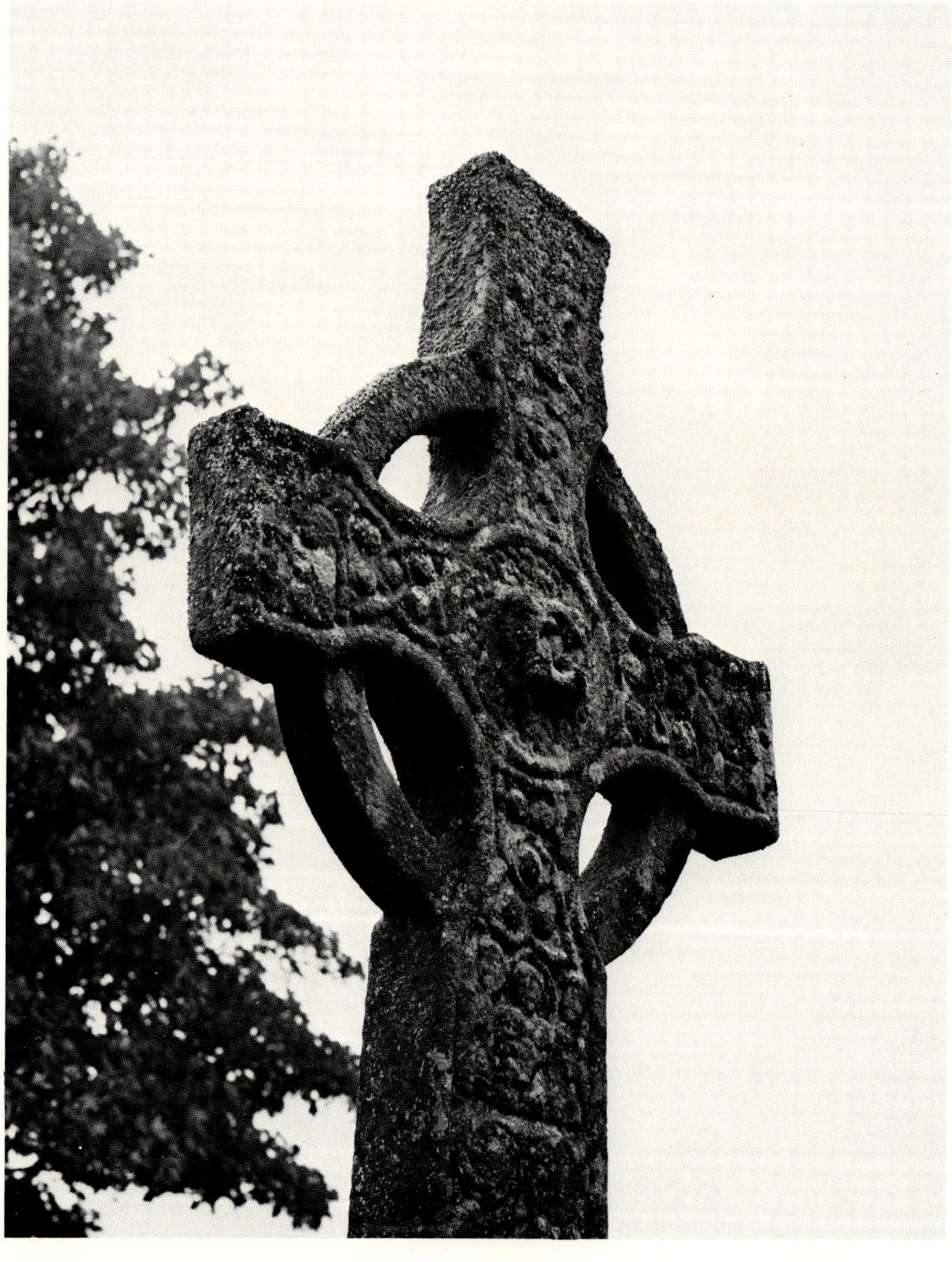

(Left) The Kildalton Cross is a finely preserved relic of the ninth century. The complex symbolism of the cross neither denies nor supplants the historic meaning of Christianity. However, aside from the usual Christian connotations, the cross also represents the tree of life and the axis of the world, important to Druidic culture.
(Above) Prior to becoming a respected Christian community, Iona was an important stronghold of Druidic culture. The cross in the foreground contains both Druidic and Christian symbolic characters.

(Above) Martyrs, kings, chieftains, warriors, and Druids sleep in peace on the island. (Right) Peaceful Iona knew its share of fighting. Warriors who fell in battle and showed great bravery were honored with stone effigies.

75

were many who remained to again rebuild the church. The final blow came on January 19, 825, when more raiders demanded the shrine, not realizing it had already been taken from the island. The abbot Blaithmac decided on passive resistance, but after mass, monks were again slaughtered. Nearly a thousand monks remained, but they too were massacred within the next few months.

Iona is honored today as much for its martyrs as for its tradition of holiness, and its indestructibility is a legend. Kings and chieftains desired to be buried in the ground where the blood of Christian martyrs had flowed. A long line of Scottish kings were laid to rest there, including Kenneth MacAlpine in 860, King Duncan in 1040—whom Shakespeare later immortalized in his tragic story of Macbeth—and Macbeth himself in 1057. On the Ridge of Kings, sixty royal personages are buried, including forty-eight Scottish, four Irish, and eight Norwegian kings. Olaf the Red, the most adventurous and feared leader of the Norsemen, fell under the spell of Iona and married the daughter of Constantine III of Scotland. Later, when thrust out of England and defeated in Ireland, he retired to Iona to live a religious life. He eventually died there, in the land that his kinsmen had defiled by their savage looting and massacres. Iona is not only a place to be visited, but a land that lives on in the memory of men.

Two decades ago, Iona was rebuilt, and its fine new cathedral again attracts spiritual pilgrims from all over the world. One of the most beautiful examples of a Celtic cross can be seen on the grounds of the new cathedral. This is the Cross of Saint Martin, which dates back to the tenth century. The Celtic cross is an ancient symbol that was known long before the coming of Christianity. Unlike the Christian version, the Celtic cross depicts the sign of harmony that we find in the union of God and the earth; its predominant meaning is conjunction. The cross proclaims the primary relationship between the two worlds, celestial and terrestrial. When the Celtic crosses were originally carved, they conveyed messages to the initiates, generally written in symbolism on the stone or stem leading to the main part of the cross. The circle around the arms of the cross represents eternal life or, in some cases, the sun, which was the primeval source of the life force.

Iona survives today, with its modern church a monument to the enduring faith of men who were prepared to die rather than yield to the forces of brute strength.

# Nine

## Islay

Islay, sometimes called the Queen of the Hebrides, is the southernmost island of the Inner Hebrides group. This group is very widely scattered off the west coast of Scotland. The main islands are Skye, Iona, Mull, Staffa, Lismore, and Islay.

The Hebrides, mentioned in the works of Ptolemy and Pliny, were first inhabited by the Celts, who were closely linked with the Druids. In the sixth century, Scandinavian hordes raced into the islands with their own northern idolatry and a lust for plundering, but in time they adopted both the language and religion of the islanders. Many exquisite examples of Celtic crosses are to be found in the Inner Hebrides, but the ninth-century Kildalton Cross on Islay is probably one of the best known. Although worn down by time and the whims of weather, a great deal of detail can still be seen.

From the dawn of man's civilization, the cross has been used both as a religious symbol and an ornament among Christian and non-Christian people alike. Thus, it may be regarded as a universal symbol that is also connected with various forms of nature worship.

The cross enclosed by a circle is a device that frequently occurs on coins and medallions of pre-Christian date, but the most dramatic ones are the stone

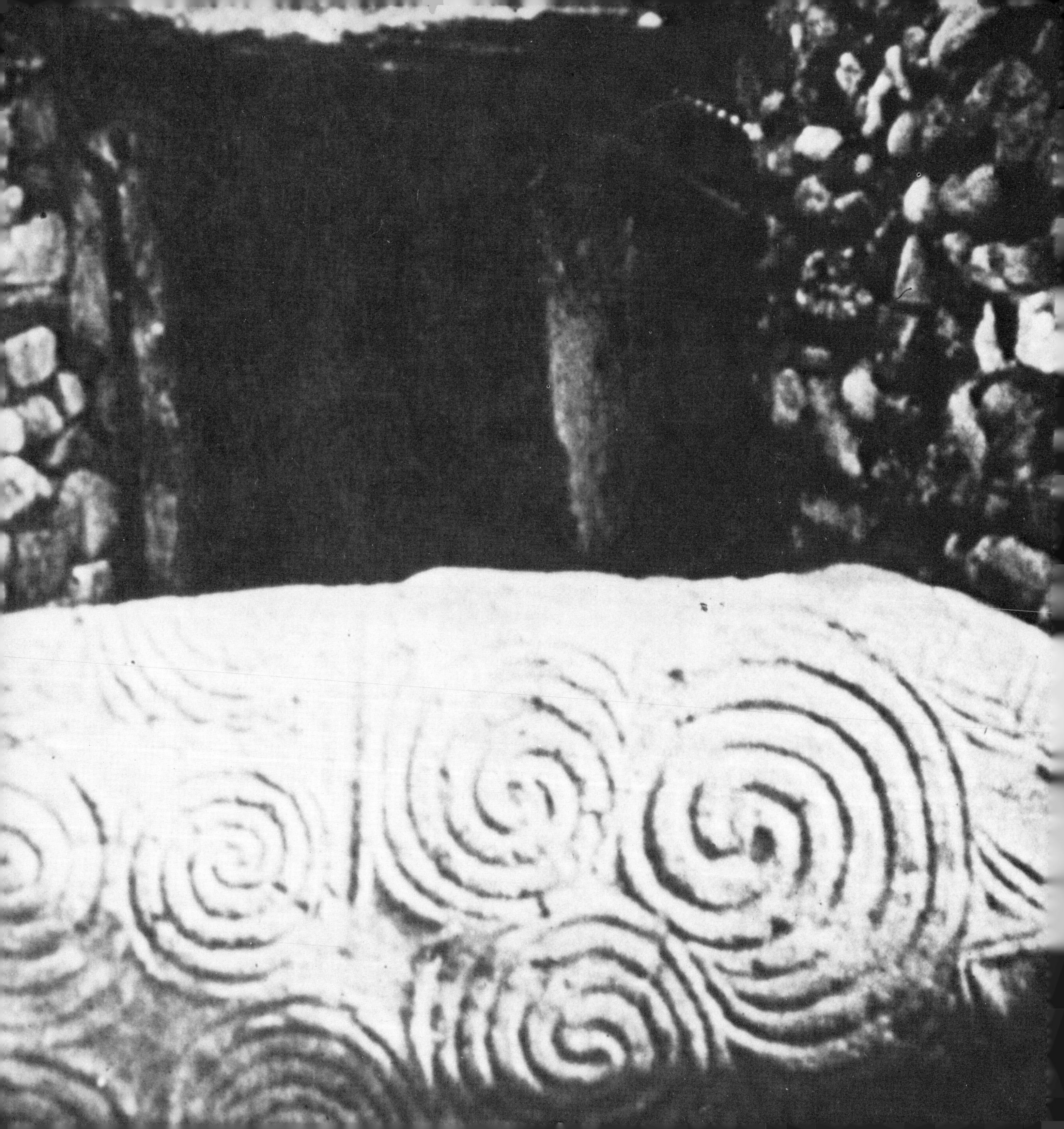

The Ogham alphabet is a form of runic writing that is found on stones, such as this one, throughout the British Isles.

Celtic crosses that mark such sacred places as Druidic circles and burial grounds. The artistic skill and ingenuity that went into the making of these early crosses produced an endless variety of singular beauty and elegance. Mixed with these attributes, the Celtic crosses exude a feeling of esoteric serenity. The four arms of the cross indicate the four elements of fire, earth, air, and water, and the circle represents cosmic consciousness, which binds all elements together.

Many of the Celtic crosses are upright standing stones inscribed with runes, which are characters of a special writing form. The Norsemen used a runic script that was said to have magical properties designed to aid or hinder, according to the motivation of the designer. This art of writing was introduced in the Iron Age.

There are three runic alphabets. The oldest one consisted of twenty-four letters, but one Scandinavian alphabet has only sixteen. The Ogham alphabet of the Druids is a form of runic alphabet. Many stones erected during the Iron Age had no inscription on them at all, and those discovered with inscriptions seem to indicate that the alphabet was only used in cases of great importance or solemnity. Some runes, however, are not strictly letters of the alphabet, but simply mystic signs that have no linguistic significance. They are more in keeping with charms or amulets in which a mysterious sign was regarded as a means of protection for the dead.

In Christian times, runes came to be regarded as an archaic curiosity and ultimately became an art form on sticks, chairs, and spoons. When we come to understand the relationship of runes to ancient religions, we will probably receive the clue to those early religions, in much the same way as the Rosetta Stone opened up the way to understanding the hieroglyphics of ancient Egypt.

# Ten

## The Isle of Arran

Arran, the largest island in the county of Bute, at the mouth of the Firth of Clyde, has been described as a miniature version of Scotland. It certainly has an affinity to the Inner Hebrides and even to Ireland, but it seems to have a unique character of its own. Standing stones, cairns, and other memorials of a remote antiquity occur in profusion, notably near Tormore, on Machrie Bay, and in Lamlash.

Brodick is the chief town of Arran, but most of the dwelling houses have been built near the pier at Invercloy. Three miles south by road is Lamlash, so completely sheltered by Holy Island that it has become an excellent harbor. Holy Island forms a natural breakwater to the Bay of St. Molios. The bay takes its name from a disciple of Saint Columba who founded a church on its northwestern point. There is a cave on the shore where Saint Molios is said to have slept on a rocky ledge. When he died, his remains were interred in the village of Clachan.

The most famous name in the history of Arran is that of Robert the Bruce, King of Scotland from 1306 to 1329, who found refuge in the King's Caves on the western coast of the island. In Glen Coy, the ruins of a fort bear the name of Bruce's Castle; here, his men lay concealed before battle.

Provokingly beautiful, every tree, mountain, and loch on the Isle of Arran seems to provide a link with the rich and romantic, but often ruthless, history of Scotland.

The early Christian saints sailed through dangerous waters to land on the rocky coastline of Arran.

Arran has been a haven for archaeologists, with its collection of chambered cairns dating back to the Mesolithic period of 5000–3000 B.C. The first comprehensive study of chambered cairns was made by Thomas Bryce for the first volume of *The Book of Arran*, published by the Arran Society of Glasgow in 1910. The most remote and the least disturbed by time is the Cairn Ban, 950 feet above sea level on the side of the Alt an t-Sluice, flowing into Kilmory Water. This chamber is eighteen-and-a-half feet long, with a breadth of three feet and a height of nine feet. The subterranean interior is divided into four almost equal compartments, separated by slabs of stone. The cairn has a forecourt with only one upright slab remaining, but there is some evidence that the cairn was once surrounded by a circle of stones.

Bryce also explored the Giant's Cave at Whiting Bay and the cairns of East Bennan and Sliddery. Archaeology has made a lot of progress since Bryce explored his cairns, but many of his ideas are still accepted, such as the premise that skeletons found in the chambers belonged to a dark-complexioned people, small in stature with long heads. He called these the Eurafrican skeletons, but his idea that they came from the southeast Mediterranean is now doubted. However, the fact that certain types of pottery found in the graves of Arran relate very closely to the same type of pottery found in the southeastern area of the Mediterranean makes his theory appear more realistic. Bryce concluded that these people came from the Iberian peninsula, but it is more likely that they came by way of the south of France to establish themselves in the Cotswold area of Britain, then moved across the Irish Sea to Ireland and finally to Arran, Bute, and Islay.

That the cairns, or horned grave passages, have a deep religious significance cannot be doubted. The cairns were small replicas of Neolithic homesteads belonging to a people who believed that the dead must be securely housed. In Egypt, the mastaba tombs built for the pharaohs between 3200 and 2780 B.C. were imitation palaces where the Egyptian rulers could live on after

At sunset, the lonely menhir on Bredda Head is a silhouetted guardian, as silent now as it was when monks and Norsemen came to Arran centuries ago.

85

death, surrounded by members of their family and many material accoutrements. The mastaba tomb was succeeded by the pyramid, a symbolic staircase on which the dead could ascend to heaven; after a funeral service of twelve hours, symbolizing the hours of darkness, the dead could reach the heavens to greet the sun at dawn.

However, the people laid to rest in the chambered cairns were buried in a fetal position, and the structure of the trapezoidal chambers may have symbolized the stomach, the forecourt the vulva, and the chamber itself the womb. In this way, entombment in the cairn could have been considered a prelude to rebirth, thus fostering the idea that the early inhabitants of Arran had some concept of reincarnation.

Thomas Bryce also conducted a systematic survey of Bronze Age burials. He found single bodies in short cisterns made of stone and covered with slabs. Some of these single internments were marked with a monolith, others were set in a stone circle, but all contained food, weapons, and implements, as well as the bodily remains. Bryce found too that cremation was practiced, after which the bones and ashes were put into pottery urns.

The stone circles of Arran have a link with Stonehenge, so it is probable that Arran knew something of the Druidic culture. (However, Arran never retained any deep interest in Druidism, probably because the island was too accessible to Ireland and England.) The calendrical significance of some of the stone circles is obvious, while those on Machrie Moor and Aucheleffan have their stones oriented to the cardinal points of the compass. Other stone circles provided the arena for ritual dancers, according to folklore and anthropological evidence. The existence of trilithons, complete with capstones through which two persons can pass, indicates that fertility dances were also common. In these dances, each couple would pass through the stones as they mimed the act of birth; through sympathetic magic, they could ensure that their union would be fruitful.

In A.D. 545, St. Brendan, during his voyage to the western islands, founded a monastery on Arran. The cashel at Kilpatrick was one of the earliest outposts of Celtic Christianity, even predating Iona. There are many ancient

This is the enchanting view between the islands of Lewis and Harris, looking toward Loch Seaforth.

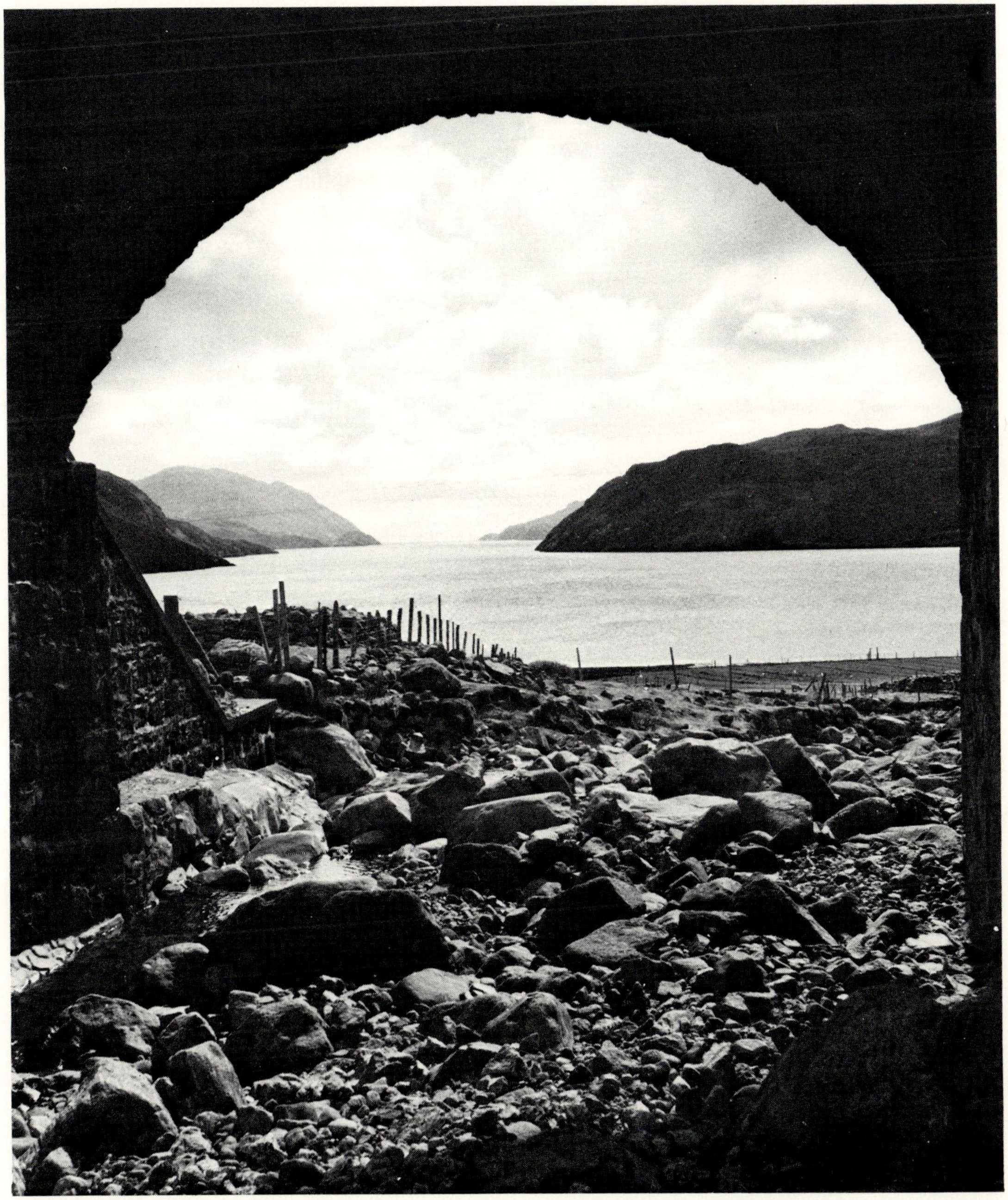

churches on Arran, and a guide to their antiquity lies in their names. It is safe to presume that all those with "kil" in the name—derived from "cill," meaning cell—belong to the early Celtic Church. It was a common practice for monks to leave the Irish monasteries and set up "cillean," or cells, on the neighboring islands. We find ecclesiastic sites at Kilpatrick, Kilmory, Kilbride Bennan, Kildonan, Kilbride, and Kilmichael. Sites without "kil" as part of the place name belong to the later Roman Church period.

Like all the other islands, especially on the west coast of Britain, Arran existed through a period when the Vikings came and plundered the island. These Norse raiders found a home there for a long time after the defeat of Haakon V at Largs in 1263. Many Vikings mated with women of the island, and there arose a mixed population deriving its language and traditions from its Gaelic-speaking mothers. For several hundred years thereafter, the inhabitants of the island retained a dual loyalty to the old Celtic gods and the God of Christianity.

From the twelfth century onward, Arran was involved in many political intrigues brought into play by conflicts between the established church and civil power. By the mid-1800's, the people of the island felt insecure because of the iniquities of patronage practiced by the ruling Dukes of Hamilton, who installed ministers of their own choosing in various churches. In 1843, the people's growing resentfulness culminated in a period called The Disruption. Members of the Church of Scotland walked out of the General Assembly and established their own Free Church, channeling a number of civil grievances into an ecclesiastical protest. As the wave of religious fanaticism swept through the island, some of the bitterness turned inward, pitting families against each other. In retrospect, the troubles in Arran seem like a preview of the same type of political and religious intrigue that has beset Northern Ireland today.

Despite its conflicts, Arran has become a favorite spot for tourists in the last two hundred years. Sir Walter Scott stimulated interest in the island when he published *The Lord of the Isles*. Many other authors have felt the spell of ancient Arran, writing always about its magical past—a past locked away in the stone circles, standing stones, and caves where religious men once prayed.

# Eleven

## Benbecula

Four large islands make up the southern chain of the Outer Hebrides: Barra, North and South Uist, and Benbecula. Each is separated from the others by a narrow channel of water, but Benbecula can be forded at low tide, when the island is harnessed to North and South Uist. Since 1941, there has been a bridge that affords some consolation to the not-so-brave traveler, whose timidity at wading through the water is well-founded. Even though a large cairn marks the path of the ford, the waters can be hazardous to those who do not appreciate how quickly the tides come in. Moreover, in Celtic lore, a ford is a favorite meeting place for ghosts. Hence, it is not unusual even today for a native of the islands to sing as he goes through the ford; as everyone knows, a voice uplifted in song will drive any ghost away.

It is only since World War II that Benbecula has become accessible to the rest of the world. Today, British Airways flies planes four times a week from Renfrew, near Glasgow, to the island. The two-hour journey is exhilarating as the plane breaks through silver and lavender clouds to give glimpses of pale golden sands below, looking like a shining wasteland until one sees the huge waves breaking on the beach.

Until 1941, travelers to Benbecula had to wait until low tide to go through the ford to reach the island. The new bridge, visible in the background, is less hazardous to today's travelers.

A view of Barra, one of the four large islands that make up the southern chain of the Outer Hebrides.

A visitor to Barra can walk among the stone ruins of Barra Castle.

The early Christian church has not withstood the storms as well as have the gravestones marking the burial place of members of the MacDonald clan of Nunton.

The burial place of the rebel lords of the Isles, the MacDonalds of Nunton, is on Benbecula, and in the desolate cemetery, Celtic and Christian crosses rise like frozen ghosts when the heavy mists shroud them in a damp cloak.

Superstitions and magic still have their place on Benbecula. Visitors may sometimes be startled by strangely disjointed sounds coming from the seashore, which blend uncannily with the shrieks of curlews. The sounds are likely to come from a seafaring man who believes he is putting a spell on the sea to bring in a good catch of herrings. If you make a tour of the island, start from the south—especially if you are visiting friends—for everyone will tell you that only witches travel from the north!

Despite the superstitions and examples of sympathetic magic, a bewildering number of faiths thrive in the Outer Hebrides. Barra is a stronghold of Roman Catholicism, but Benbecula has always remained a neutral zone, tolerant of fervent Catholics as well as Presbyterian ministers. Benbecula is only sixty miles from the sacred island of Iona, from which sixth-century missionaries carried Christianity to pagan Scotland. Yet unlike the other islands, Benbecula's isolation was never encroached upon by strong missionary forces. Perhaps it is good to have a neutral religious zone in this remote part of the world.

Stone wheelhouses, such as the one shown here, were popular in Scotland during the Iron Age but were known to be in existence during the Roman period as well. They were built circular in shape, with partition walls projecting like the spokes of a wheel. Evidence of wheelhouses in South Uist indicates that the island knew long years of peace, since this type of homestead was mainly occupied in between wars.

# Twelve

## St. Kilda

St. Kilda is the largest of a small group of islets in the Outer Hebrides. Viewed from the shores of Uist, these tiny islands seem like the pillars of a ruined fortress rising from the ocean.

The Gaelic name of this island was Hirta, meaning "the western land." The origin of its present name, however, is as ghostly as the island itself, for no saint was ever named Kilda.

Until recently, the island was inaccessible for eight months of the year, but now ships cruise between the islands of the Outer Hebrides. A small segment of St. Kilda is leased to the Ministry of Defense to accommodate military personnel employed in tracing guided missiles fired from South Uist. Military personnel seem to outnumber the natives, for the geographical isolation forced many inhabitants to emigrate.

Dominating the island is Conachair, which must surely be one of the most awe-inspiring cliffs in all the British Isles. The volcanic structures are a challenge to any rock climber, but the inhabitants of St. Kilda scale them regularly in search of sea birds. It takes courage and strength to capture puffins, fulmar petrels, razorbills, Manx shearwaters, and solan geese, but the islanders depend on these birds for food and oil.

The islanders have very definite Norse characteristics: long aquiline noses, well-marked eyebrows, well-built bodies of medium height. The early St. Kildans lived in subterranean circular dwellings that provided the necessary warmth in winter. By 1838, houses were constructed of rough stones with walls from five to eight feet thick. Many scholarly visitors to the island have been intrigued with the structure of Kildan houses throughout the centuries.

Prior to 1779, the island was in the possession of the MacLeod clan. The chief of that time sold it, but it was repurchased for $10,000 by another MacLeod in 1781. Succeeding generations of MacLeods refused permission for strangers to buy land, and so the population dwindled.

Donald Munro, High Dean of the Isles, visited the Hebrides in 1549 and mentioned St. Kilda in his records. He found the inhabitants "simple, poor and scarce learnt in any religion," but he was applying Christian standards to his analysis. For several centuries before Munro's visit, the religion was based on Druidic principles, which in due course became interlaced with Popery. In 1641, Colla Ciotach of the MacDonald clan visited the island several times, where it is said "he employed himself in teaching the natives the Lord's Prayer, the Decalogue and the Creed, all in the Popish style." In 1697, Martin Martin visited St. Kilda, about which Lachlan Maclean wrote in 1838:

> *Martin Martin was to them another Knox, in throwing down their altars and scourging their will-worship. They believed in God the Father, the Son and the Holy Ghost, but also in Flathinnis, the island of the brave, and Iibhroin, the region of sorrow. They rose in the morning and commenced their labor by invoking the name of God and swearing was not known amongst them.*

In 1705, the General Assembly of the Church of Scotland considered the St. Kildans to be in a deplorable state of spiritual awareness. As a result, Alexander Buchan was sent there to help nourish the spirit of the islanders. During his ministry, he built the first manse and started a library, while his wife taught the native women how to knit. When Buchan died in 1730, St. Kilda seems to have been left to its own devices as far as religion was concerned, but in 1758, a series of ministers again went to the island. By 1822, there was no sign of the original manse; neither was there an organized church with any semblance of the Calvinist religion.

The Reverend John MacDonald paid his first visit to the island in 1822 and laid the foundations for a highly organized, harsh and puritanical religion.

MacDonald, who became known as the Apostle of the North, wrote of that time:

> *Swearing is too prevalent among them and its common expressions, such as by the soul, by Mary, by the book . . . and what is worse, by the sacred name, seem to be quite familiar with them on every occasion. It grieves me to say and I took pains to ascertain the truth that among the whole body, I did not find a single individual who could be truly called a decidedly religious person.*

St. Kilda again became a spiritual challenge, and after frequent visits to the island, the Reverend MacDonald left it to the care of the Reverend Neil MacKenzie in 1830. For fourteen years, he ministered to the needs of the natives, softening the harsh puritanical approach by trying to raise their standard of living. For the next ten years, the St. Kildans were under the care of a catechist, Duncan Kennedy, who was in turn succeeded by the Reverend Camwron. The island then came under the sway of the Reverend John MacKay, who was specially ordained to take over the ministry of the island. His incumbency was a tough one, lasting twenty-four years, during which he pressed the islanders too hard and incurred the literary wrath of two writers, John Sands and Robert Connell. Sands wrote of MacKay:

> *The weak-minded Pope and Prime Minister rolled into one who rules the destinies of the island has reduced religion into a mere hypocritical formalism, finding no place in his creed for self reliance or any of the manlier virtues. It is nothing to Mr. MacKay whether the poor people starve their crofts or neglect fishing so long as his own silly fads are observed.*

MacKay forgot that life on St. Kilda was in itself a sort of religious experience, in that it required a strong faith for anyone to remain on the rugged island.

It seems to have been the fate of St. Kilda to bear the brunt of a series of unimaginative men whose bigotry darkened the pages of history. Such men could not understand the traditions and folklore that had been instilled for a dozen generations in the native St. Kildans. Close to nature, they knew a great deal about survival in all its terms, whether physical, mental, or spiritual. Hellfire and damnation could never be a creed in which they could realize their innermost yearnings, or the spiritual experience of higher consciousness; this they found in their everyday way of life.

Folklore is the survival of the thoughts and ways of life of former times, preserved mostly by verbal communication. In such a small, well-insulated community as St. Kilda, where personal survival was always the order of the day, old folktales remained intact and impervious to new religious ideas. St. Kilda is steeped in Norse legends of heroes who survived the elements, conquering water and earth, aided by the supernatural force of fairies and other guardians of the island.

Belief in the supernatural on St. Kilda is associated with the Clach an Eolas, the "stone of knowledge." If a man stood on the stone of knowledge on the first day of the quarter, he would receive second sight and be able to look into the future. Another stone that features prominently in the island's tradition is the Clach Dotaig—the "stone of virtue"—a semi-transparent stone held in reverence by the islanders. To obtain the stone of virtue, a person had to boil the egg of a raven and then return it to the nest. The parent bird, becoming impatient when the egg did not hatch, would oust this "stone" from the nest, and the person who chanced upon it could be sure that he had a treasured supernatural possession. The raven is linked with the symbolism of both the Druids and the Norsemen, who believed that the universe itself was a sacred egg.

Several accounts written about St. Kilda mention that sacrifices were once offered to the god of the seasons on a rock called the Mullach-geal. Until the eighteenth century, St. Kildans poured libations of milk on a stone near the village of Hirt that was associated with the supernatural being called the Grugach. This was done to ensure a good supply of milk from the cattle, an important necessity to the islanders who would also pray for blessings on their cattle. Grazing grounds were sanctified with salt, water, and fire before cattle were allowed to feed on them. Such old beliefs in sympathetic magic do not die away, and so it is no wonder the Christian missionaries found St. Kilda a tough place to totally Christianize.

There are several supernatural wells on St. Kilda, a carry-over from the belief in animism that was widespread before the advent of Christianity. Tobar na Buadh was considered the "well of virtue," where the water was a sovereign cure for a great variety of ailments. The well was famous when Martin Martin visited the island, and he recorded that it was "the finest of the excellent fountains or springs in which St. Kilda abounds." Another famous well, called the Tobar na Cille in Gaelic, was dedicated to Saint Brendanbut. When the winds were too rough for the men to launch their boats, the direction of the wind could be altered if a man stood astride the well waters for a few minutes.

Probably one of the most interesting tidbits of folklore on the island is the exclusive legend of "the Amazon." Her house is still known today as the Tigh na Banaghaisgich, or "House of the Female Warrior." Again the indefatigable recorder of his times was Martin Martin, whose description of the house is graphic and picturesque:

*Upon the west side of the Isle lies a valley with a declination towards the sea, with a rivulet running through the middle of it, on each side of which is an ascent of half a mile. All which piece of ground is called by the inhabitants, The Female Warrior's Glen. This Amazon is famous in their traditions. Her house or Dairy of Stone is yet extant and it is in the form of a circle. Pyramidwise towards the top with a vent in it, the fire being always in the center of the floor. The body of this house contains not above nine persons sitting; there are three beds, or low vaults at the side of the wall; at each entry to one of these low vaults is a stone standing upon one end. Upon this she is reported ordinarily to have laid her helmet. There are two stones on the one side, upon which she is said to have laid her sword. They tell you that she was much addicted to hunting and that in her days all the space betwixt this isle and that of Harris was one continued tract of dry land.*

From this report of 1697, the Amazon was probably the St. Kildan version of Diana the Huntress, the goddess of the moon. In which case, St. Kilda is likely to have been at one time under a matriarchal system of government.

The structures around the House of the Female Warrior comprise two "horned" structures, each with its own court. On the south side, there are evidences of stone avenues, small circles, and monoliths, which would suggest that an ancient witch coven met here to perform rituals of magic. It is surprising that this area of Gleann Mor has never been subjected to scientific investigation, for it could present a real challenge to a professional archaeologist. Ultimately, these stone relics may prove to be a vital link with the female division of Druidism, of which existing witch covens in Europe are an intrinsic part even today.

# Thirteen

## Boreray

Some four miles northeast of St. Kilda lies Boreray, which even in good weather is a difficult island to land on. Based on archaeological finds, this tiny speck in the Atlantic Ocean links well with the idea that St. Kilda was the ancient hideaway of a strong body of matriarchal rulers as well as Druidic forces.

A recent investigation of the megalithic sites of Britain produced the idea that the summit of Boreray was used as a calendar marker in association with the menhirs erected *circa* 1790 B.C. on the Outer Hebrides. These menhirs include the standing stones of An Carra on South Uist, an oriented stone on Benbecula, Clach an t-Sagait on North Uist, and Clach Mhic-Leoid on Harris. It is not a coincidence that all these stones are oriented toward Boreray with complete accuracy, for when the sun sets behind Boreray, each of these gives primary calendar declinations. This would suggest a link with the Druids, who we know were obsessed with working out the arrangements of such declinations.

On Boreray, there is also the Staller's House, meaning "Stone Man's House," about which Martin Martin remarked:

*In the west of this island is Staller House, which is much larger than that of the female warrior of St. Kilda, but of much the same model in all respects; it is all green without, like a little hill.*

The English historian and author Thomas Macaulay extends this description:

> *The structure is eighteen feet deep and its top lies almost level with the earth, by which it is surrounded; below it is of circular form and all its parts are contrived so that a single stone covers the top. If this stone is removed, the house has a very sufficient vent. In the middle of the floor is a large hearth; round the wall is a paved seat, on which sixteen people may conveniently sit. There are four roofed beds, roofed with strong flags or strong lintels, everyone of which is capable to receive four men. To each of these beds is a separate entry, the distance between these separate openings resembling, in some degree, so many pillars.*

Although the structure is now in a ruined state, local people say that there is an entrance from the house leading to a sea cave seven hundred feet below it. We are of the opinion that at one time, an underwater passage gave the females of St. Kilda access to the Staller's House, where the Stone Men were in charge of specific religious duties related to observing the heavens.

On nearby Soay Island, there is a similar type of structure, but there is evidence that this one contained an altar. It is probable that both sexes met here for various seasonal religious purposes. If this is a fact, then Boreray would have been the observatory where the males worked, St. Kilda the domain of the females versed in hunting and the functions of looking after their community, and Soay the sacred ground used exclusively for religious rituals.

Boreray is also called "the north island," which again relates to Druidism and witchcraft, for it is from the north that witches make their entrances.

Carved in stone, this Pictish cross resembles a swastika, which in ancient times symbolized life and vigor.

# Fourteen

## Callanish Standing Stones: The Isle of Lewis

They stand like sentinels jealously guarding a secret treasure, thirteen tall pillars of stone, desolate on the bleak moorland—mute frozen relics erected some two thousand years before the birth of Christ.

The Callanish Standing Stones, located on the Isle of Lewis in the Outer Hebrides, are a superb example of what must have been an important Druidic structure. There are now only thirteen pillars forming a circle, within which is a chamber with its entrance near the tallest pillar rising fifteen-and-a-half feet above the earth.

The stones are approached by an avenue of some quarter-of-a-mile in length, an avenue that once was lined with other tall stones, of which only nine now remain. Anyone who stands in the center of the circle can see that there was originally a single line of four stones extending from east to west, and a single line of five other stones stretching to the south. Viewed from the north end of the avenue, the design is that of a cross.

There are several legends about the origin of these stones. One tells the story of a priest who came to the island in a ship containing huge stones and of black-skinned men who erected them. But this legend is far removed from the truth because the standing stones are huge, undressed blocks of gneiss, and this

The Callanish Standing Stones are a superb example of what was once a Druidic temple, probably as important as Stonehenge.

The massive stones presented a great challenge to those who engineered them into position.

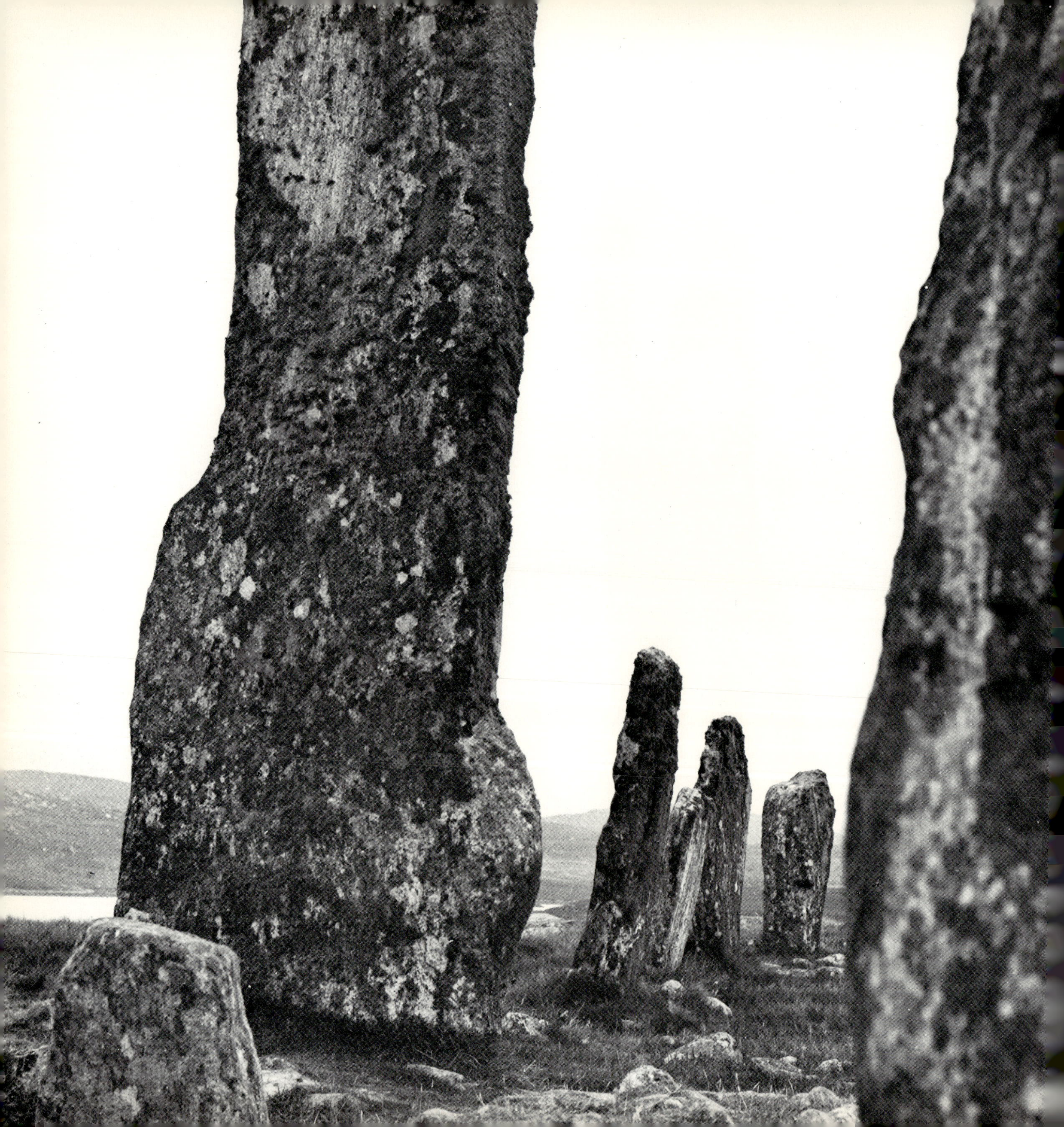

These tall pillars are the remains of the long avenue of stones that led to the inner circle, where sacred rituals were performed by the Druids.

particular rock is the main structure of the island itself. It is more likely that when the Druids came to the island, they made use of the local material in their usual practical manner.

Another legend says that when the first notes of the cuckoo were heard and as the sun rose at dawn, the figure of the "Shining One" could be seen walking down the avenue toward the circle. The cuckoo is a bird sacred to Celtic lore.

Still another legend states that when Saint Kirian arrived on Lewis to start a Christian community, he found the island inhabited by giants who held regular councils at Callanish. It is likely that Saint Kirian found the Druids there, and because they were able to change their shape through magic, he saw them as giants. The inhabitants refused to help him build a new church dedicated to the Christian faith, and so he changed them into stone. Whenever a missionary expedition followed the Druids to one of the outer islands, there is always a record that the Druids refused to help and did all they could to thwart the building of Christian churches. Once again, in the Isle of Lewis, we find a reiteration of the idea that Druidic magic was confronted by Christian magic throughout the British Isles.

To stand in the center of the Callanish Standing Stones is to experience a strong flow of psychic energy even today.

# Fifteen

## The Orkneys

Night seems to come reluctantly to the Orkneys, sending an advance force of lengthening shadows as if hesitant to let the pale shafts of sunshine drown in the waters of Kirkwall Bay. Seagulls soar through fluffy grey clouds until they become tinged with a rosy hue, giving the illusion of phantom flamingoes incongruous in the alien setting of rocks and crags.

At midsummer, night in its turn is hunted by the sun, resplendent in golden glory until after midnight. Yet it is as the day slips into nightfall that the bleakness of the Orkneys is subdued into a ghostly beauty, strangely tidy in contrast to the rest of the Scottish Islands.

In daytime, one sees rolling hills, bare and gaunt at the top, which then slide into a sweet greenness and finally dive into the expanses of heather treacherously hiding the peat below. The absence of trees is startling to a newcomer, and what few there are appear on the landscape like deformed arthritic gnomes, all leaning eastward to escape the westerly winds. The lush greenness comes from the rain, which torments with its impetuous starts and then defies frustration and despair by clearing up, admitting sharp shafts of sunlight to again transform the scene.

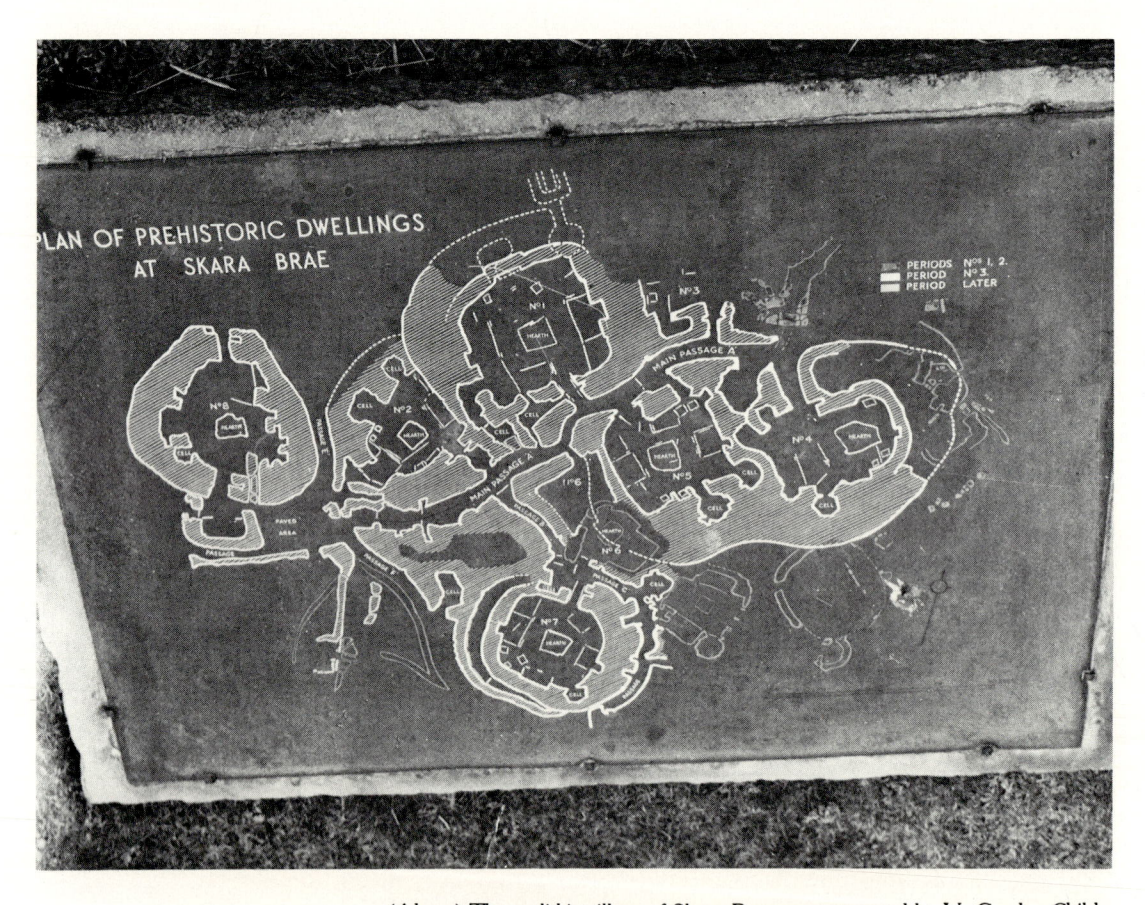

(Above) The neolithic village of Skara Brae was excavated by V. Gordon Childe in 1928-30. The village consisted of several houses and a workshop, all linked together by alleyways. These alleys were paved over, and in time, the entire village was literally buried under layer after layer of refuse. (Right) Because of the lack of timber on the island, the houses and internal furnishings were made of stone. Dry-stone wall building is still a unique art in the Orkneys.

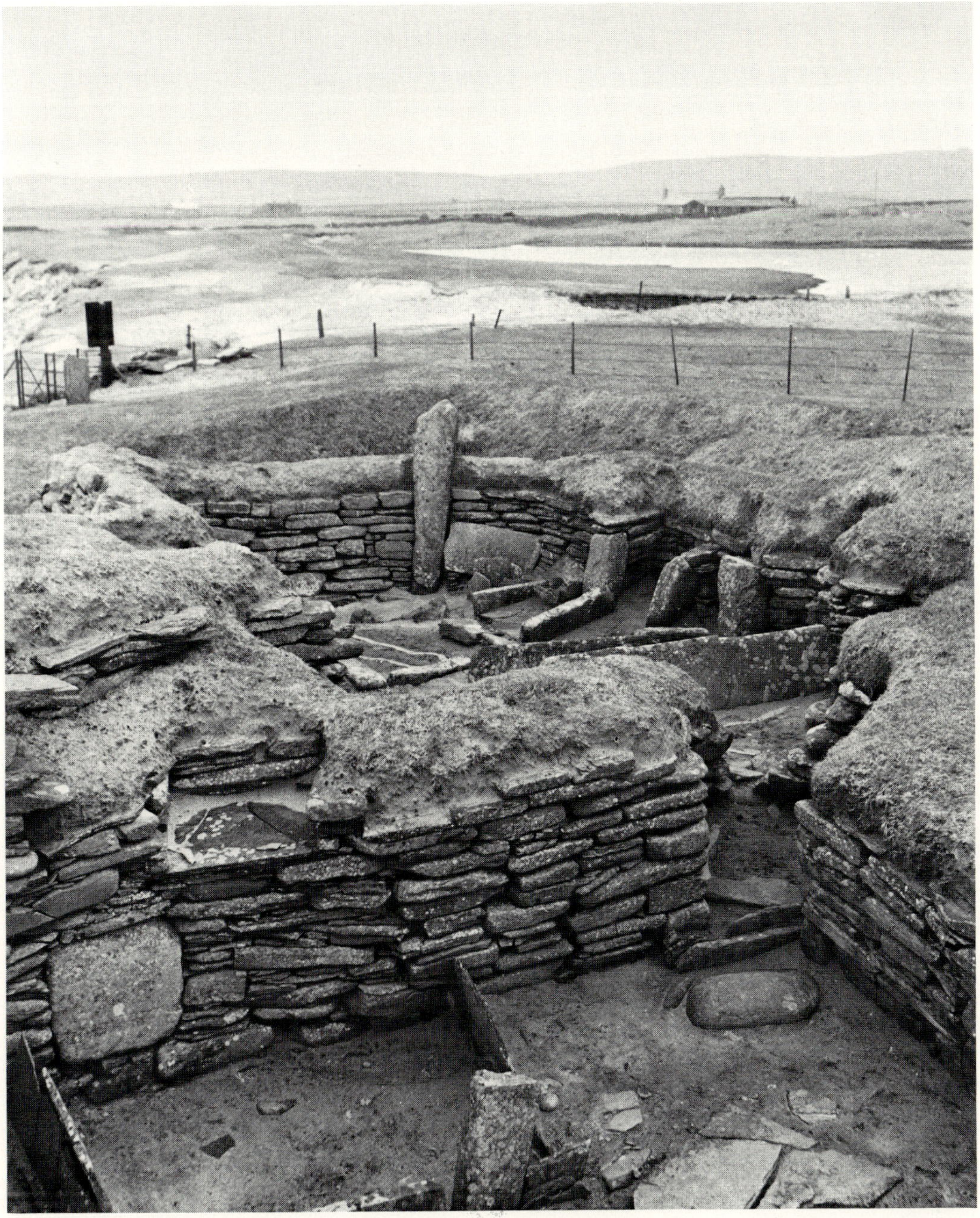

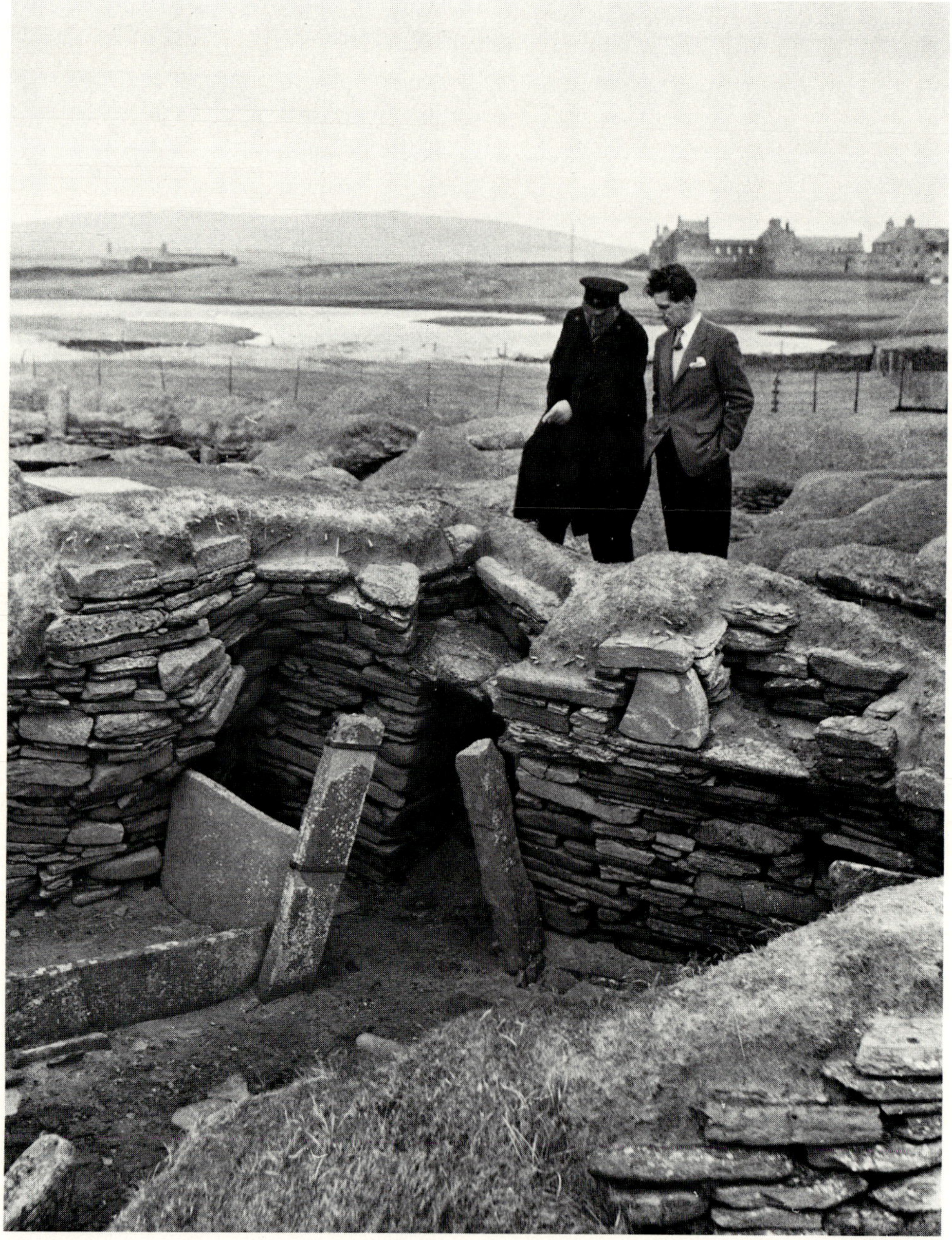

Everything about the Orkneys is a surprise, sometimes coaxing, cajoling, and consoling a visitor, then striking fear into his heart with the supernatural sense of history as he looks at landmarks that had religious significance in earlier times—landmarks such as the Old Man of Hoy, the Stack of Yesnaby, and Maeshowe, the ancient burial ground of chambered tombs near Stromness.

The Orkneys were originally the Orcades, beloved of ancient classical writers, and the earliest inhabitants were the Picts. Evidence of their unique way of life still exists in numerous "weems" or subterranean houses, in chambered mounds, barrows, and burial grounds, in "brochs" or round towers, and in stone circles and standing stones. The Picts remained in power into the seventh century, when marauding Norsemen arrived in longboats to establish a foothold on the islands. These men gave the Orkneys a Golden Age all their own and a romantic ancestry to most of the families still on the islands. The Orcadians are first and foremost Orcadians, and Scottish afterward. The islands only became part of Scotland in 1468 when they were given away by the King of Denmark, Christian I, as part of the marriage dowry of his daughter, Margaret, when she married James III of Scotland.

In the twelfth century, however, the Vikings plundered the burial grounds at Maeshowe and spent three days carting away the treasures left with the dead. They carved graffiti on the walls of the chambers, which comes as another surprise. What type of man was he who wrote "The carver of these carvings is the cleverest man in all Western Europe"? For sure, he was not lacking in a flamboyant appraisal of himself. Who was Ingibiorch? She must have been quite a woman who left a memory on one Viking, for he carved "Ingibiorch is the fairest woman of them all"—so leaving her name, if not her identity, as part of the history of the island.

The Orkneys also saw the invasion of Celtic missionaries, the companions of Saint Columba who brought Christianity to a land that knew the animistic influence of pagans and Druids. In contrast to the stone circles and standing

Neolithic man used the circle—the oldest of all shapes—as part of both his home life and his religious life.

stones—relics of a primitive but religious culture—the Cathedral of Saint Magnus dominates the skyline of the Norse town of Kirkwall, its copper spire rising gracefully to the heavens. Few of the churches and cathedrals on the Scottish islands are dedicated to saints who were canonized, and in this case, the title of "saint" was conferred upon the second son of the Earl of Magnus by the King of Norway in 1231. In this year, the Nordic title of "jarl" became extinct, except where used in place names, but the influence of the Norse language lingered until the eighteenth century.

The Orkneys were almost forgotten until the Second World War. Then on paths once trod by Druids and Celtic missionaries, Italian prisoners of war walked and worked. In October of 1939, a German U-boat crept into Scapa Flow and sent the battleship *Royal Oak* into the depths of the ocean, complete with some eight hundred men aboard. There, they joined the watery graveyard of the German Fleet, which deliberately sank seventy-five of its finest ships in June of 1919. The Orkneys, once the refuge of Druids and missionaries, provided a new type of refuge in two wars, when the proud British Naval Fleet was protected by the natural haven of Scapa Flow.

The Orkneys have always been alternately a home for religious refugees and the victim of marauders, but what remains today is the charm of their physical features, typical of other Scottish islands. What is left in the Orkneys are beautiful atmospheric effects, extraordinary examples of nuances of light and shade, mingling with the rich coloration of the cliffs and the sea. Perhaps the atmosphere of the Orkneys is not felt so much inland as by the ocean. The beautiful waters are serene and innocent one moment, and become raging spires of foam the next, as if the eternal sea remembers all the historic past of the Orkneys, its Jarlstowns and its cathedral.

Now there is another hazard coming to the Orkneys, and they may never again be the paradise that ancient classical writers glorified. The land is being raped by oilmen laying the foundations of a hundred-mile pipeline from the tiny island of Flotta. After generations of peaceful innocence, it may be the karmic

The chambered tombs found on Orkney revealed that graffiti was not unknown to our ancestors.

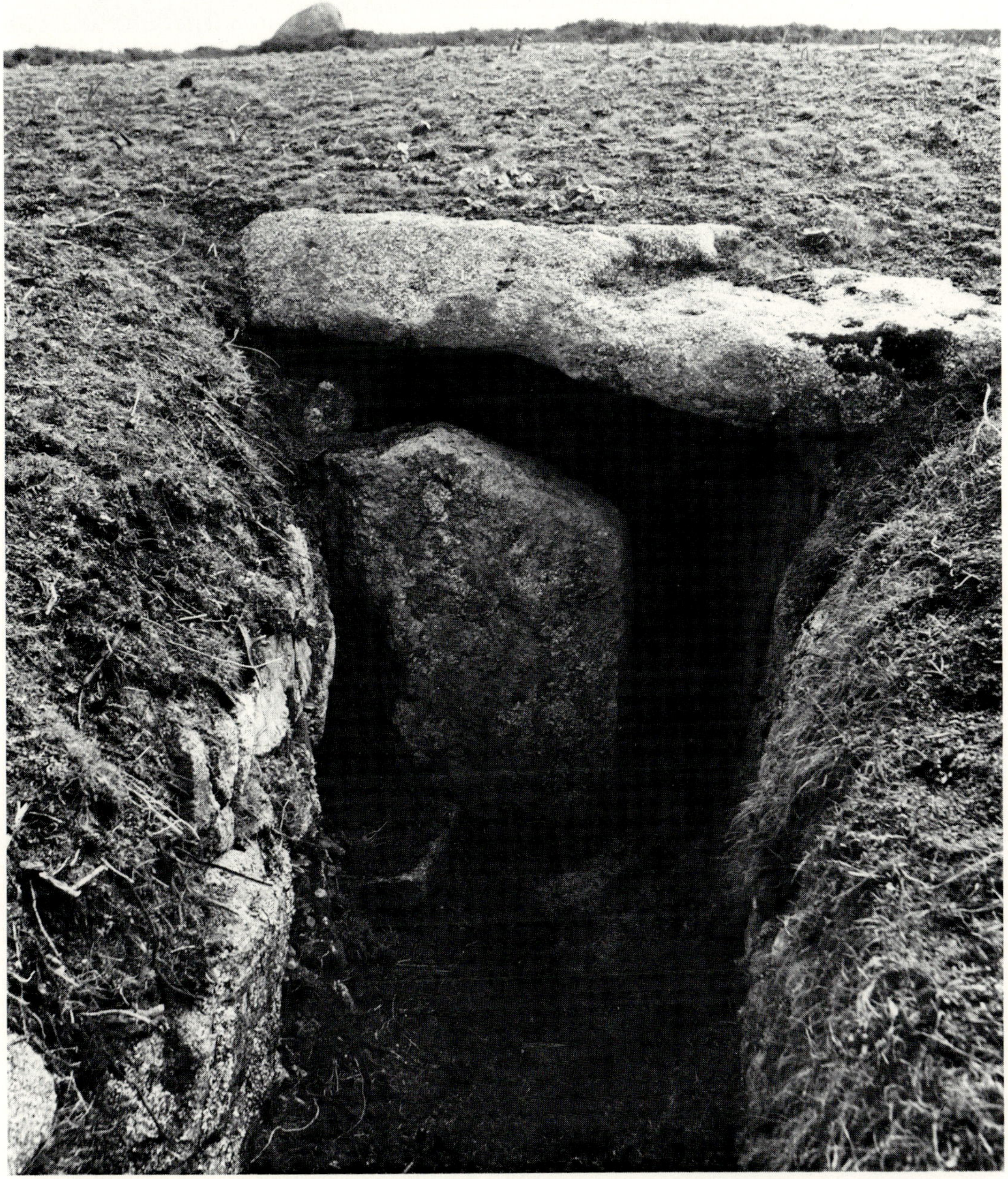

fate of the Orkneys to feel the hand of the marauding defilers once again ravaging the land and the waters around the islands. Will these invaders carve their own twentieth-century graffiti as the Norsemen did? If they do, Ingibiorch, "the fairest woman of them all," will have to share her ghostly existence with "Bud of Houston loves Debbie of Dallas."

There is hope that such islands as the Orkneys are totally indestructible. Men have come and gone, native islanders have suffered but survived, and the Old Man of Hoy, the stone circles, and the standing stones remain redolent with the nostalgia of their times, which no other time and circumstances have ever been able to erase.

# *Sixteen*

## *Lerwick: the Festival of Up-Helly-Aa*

Lerwick, a member of the Shetland group of islands, has the distinction of being the northernmost of the British Isles. It is situated on Brassey Sound, a fine natural harbor on the east coast of the island called Mainland. It is on Lerwick that one of the main fire festivals of the world is celebrated in the last days of January. This is the remarkable event called Up-Helly-Aa. Every year, a replica of a Viking longship is dragged ceremonially through the streets in a torchlight parade. When it reaches the seashore, it is set alight as the fiery torches are flung into the boat. As a spectacle for tourists, this fire festival is a unique experience.

The word "viking" means a sea pirate, of which there were many who raided the islands around Scotland and Britain. Few islands were safe from these predatory Norsemen; Iona, the Isle of Man, Ireland, Sheppey, and Holy Isle were all victims of their raids. Yet unlike many marauders, the Norsemen had their own code of honor, and while it did not show mercy to those who resisted it, the code contained specific provisions for the division of booty, and punishment for theft, desertion, and treachery.

The courage of the Vikings and their skill in sailing through rough weather and uncharted waters are well known. They were not entirely unlettered,

(Above) The splendor of the sun rivals the fiery rays of the burning longboat in the Up-Helly-Aa festival on the Isle of Lerwick. (Right) The giant figurehead is set in place as the replica of a Viking longboat is constructed.

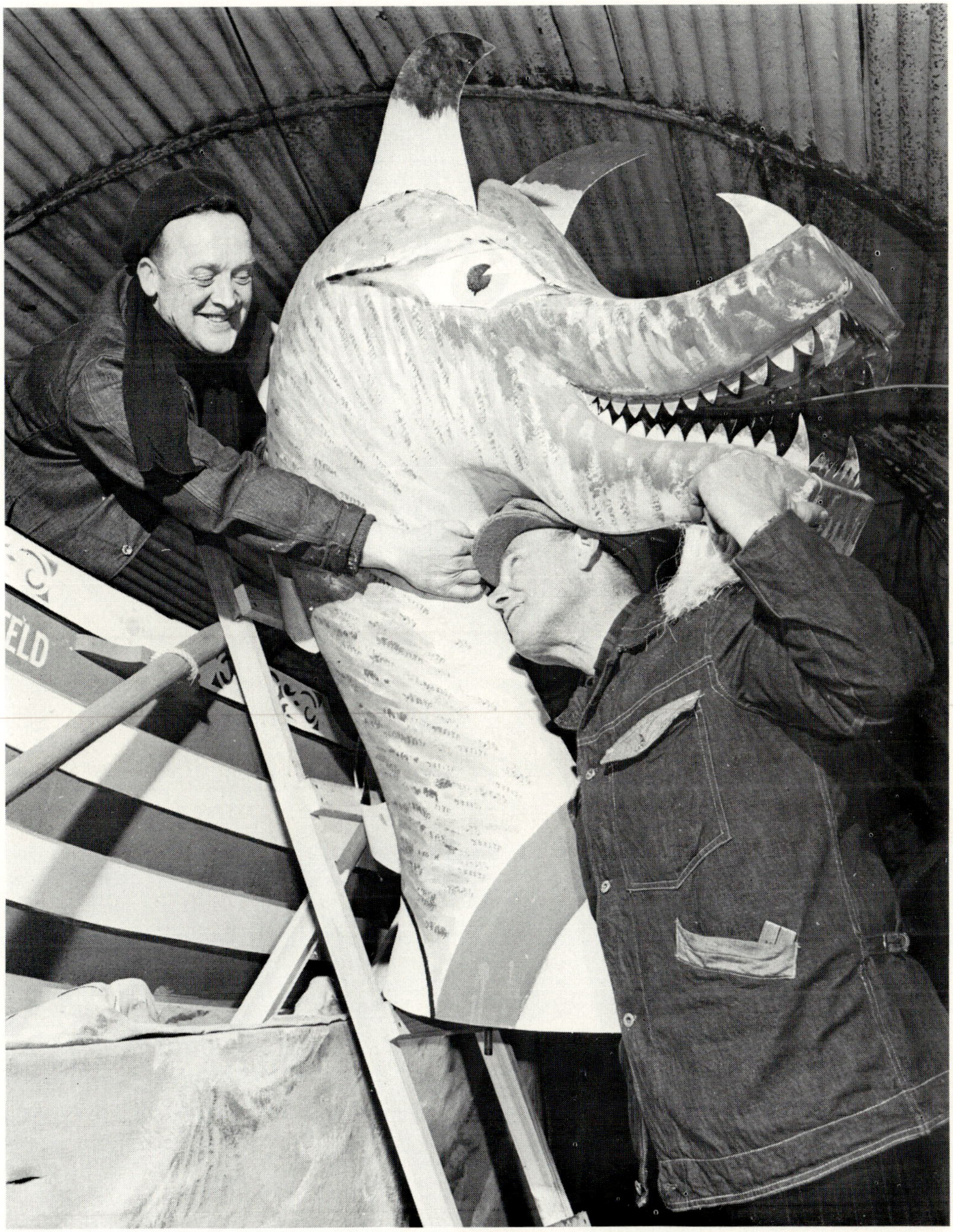

Modern-day Vikings on Lerwick stand near the Viking longboat and survey the scene for their Up-Helly-Aa festival.

In the torchlight parade, the longboat is ceremonially dragged to the ocean.

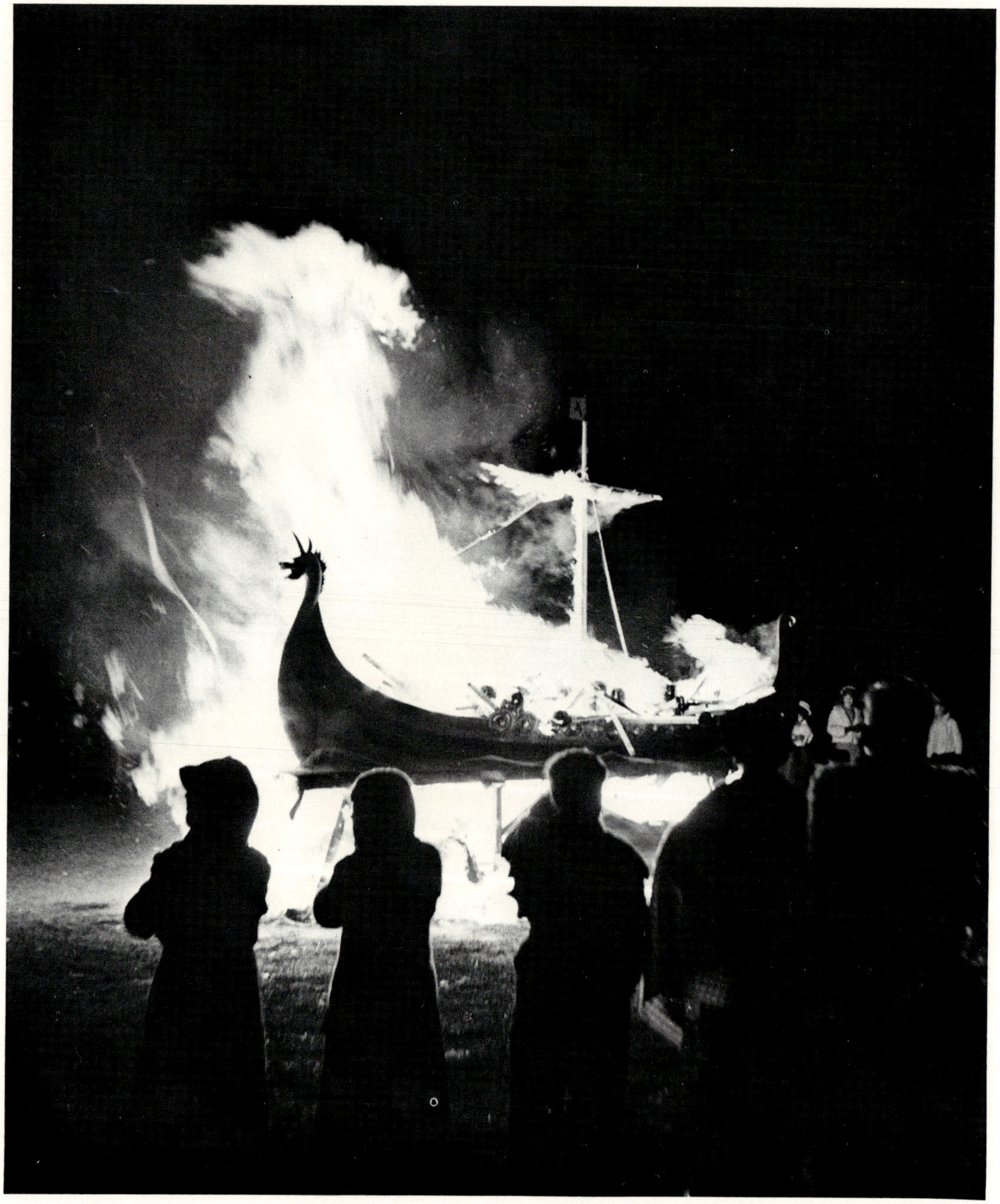

(Left) Fiery torches set the boat alight, providing a remarkable spectacle for tourists and participants alike. (Above) The giant figurehead rears in a last dying gasp before flames consume it.

and well understood the use of runes, a script that has magical properties. Norse runic script was used in initiation ceremonies to help or harm others, but mainly to keep the race healthy and to gain victory. Thus, always confident of their own magic power, the Norsemen did not fear native superstitions and were not afraid of those who also had magic. A combination of ruthless energy, strong arms to row the longboats and wield swords, and belief in the power of the runes was probably responsible for the success the Norsemen had during their lengthy well-planned raids.

Viking longboats also struck terror into the hearts of many ancient Christian communities; in the course of a generation, almost all the monastic communities of western Scotland were attacked. From the beginning of the establishment of Christian monastic centers around the British Isles, the Norsemen showed little appreciation for men of spirituality. It should not be supposed, however, that the Norsemen made their raids in order to wipe out Christianity; their main objective was to loot the monasteries of rich gold and silver. Because of the suffering inflicted on religious orders, a special prayer known as "A furore Normannorum liberanos" was inserted in many litanies.

The Vikings were not adverse to making deals with members of those Christian communities which they sacked and massacred earlier, and many received land from Christians on which they settled. In many of the northern isles, the Norsemen lived side by side with Christians. Of all the European lands, England was without a doubt that on which the Viking Age left the most impression in the number of original settlers who remained after 878.

Today, in its Up-Helly-Aa festival, Lerwick celebrates a fire festival that probably has its grass roots in the ancient Oimelc celebration. The festival culminates in the Candlemas festivities of February 2, originally celebrated by ancient Druids and witches as a festival of light. The early Christian Church kept up this festival in commemoration of the Presentation of Christ in the Temple

A Norseman watches the last rites of this sacrifice to the sun-god.

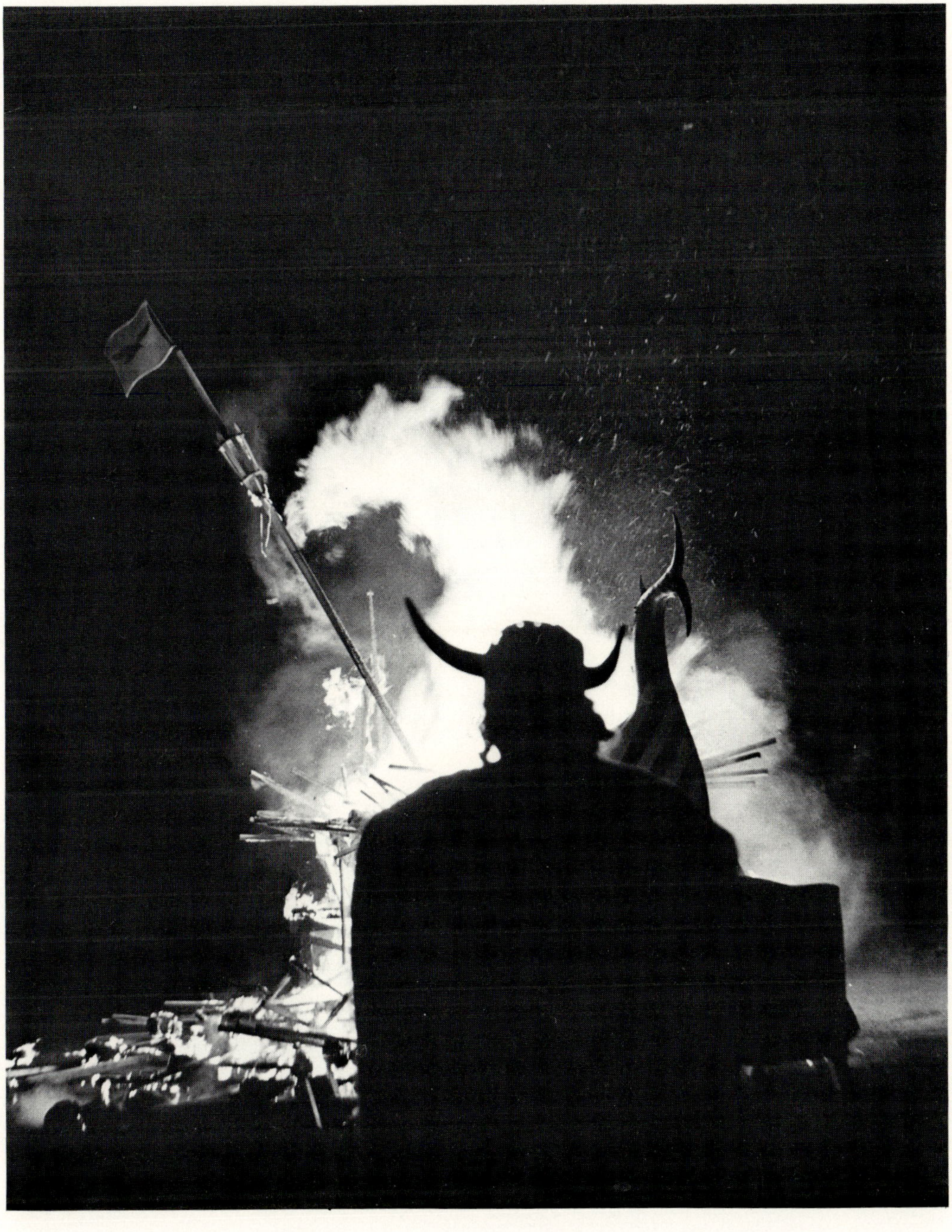

and the Purification of the Blessed Virgin. The eighth-century "Gelasian Sacramentary" mentions this festival, which leads one to presume it was ordained by Pope Gelasius I in 402 as a counterattraction to the pagan festival of Lupercalia. The customs of blessing candles for the whole year did not come into common use until the eleventh century, at which time it became known as Candlemas. The Up-Helly-Aa festival also marks the climax of midwinter, and the ritual of burning a fiery longboat relates to the pagan custom of using fire to symbolize the end of the dark days of winter and the coming of the longer days of spring when the sun again would give its life-giving rays to start a new season of fertility.

    In this festival, therefore, we find a pagan custom merging with a Christian one, as well as a long-standing revenge on the ancient pirates.

# Seventeen

## The Isle of Wight

This diamond-shaped island is a familiar landmark off the south coast of England, set like a jewel in the English Channel and worn at the slender throat of Southampton Water. A scintillating island aptly called "The Garden Isle," it is rich in scenic beauty and steeped in history.

Wight is part of the county of Hampshire, but is separated from the mainland by two waterways: the Solent and Spithead. The greatest ships of the world have steamed past the Isle of Wight, up the Solent and into the ancient port of Southampton. Because the island is in this main shipping lane, it is also within easy reach of both England and France, making it a halfway point between two great commercial centers.

The name of the island is linked with the Welsh "ynys wyth," meaning "turn," a word that cognates with the Latin name Vectis, literally meaning "the act of lifting," or "lever." When the historian Diodorus Siculus referred to "Island Ictis," he was speaking of the same island that the Gauls called Vectis.

The Isle of Wight is steeped in history from the time of the ancient Britons who brought tin to the island to export to Gaul. According to that remarkable chronicler of events, Julius Caesar, the Celts were the first inhabitants of Wight. The Belgae, a Germanic-Celtic tribe, colonized the island *circa*

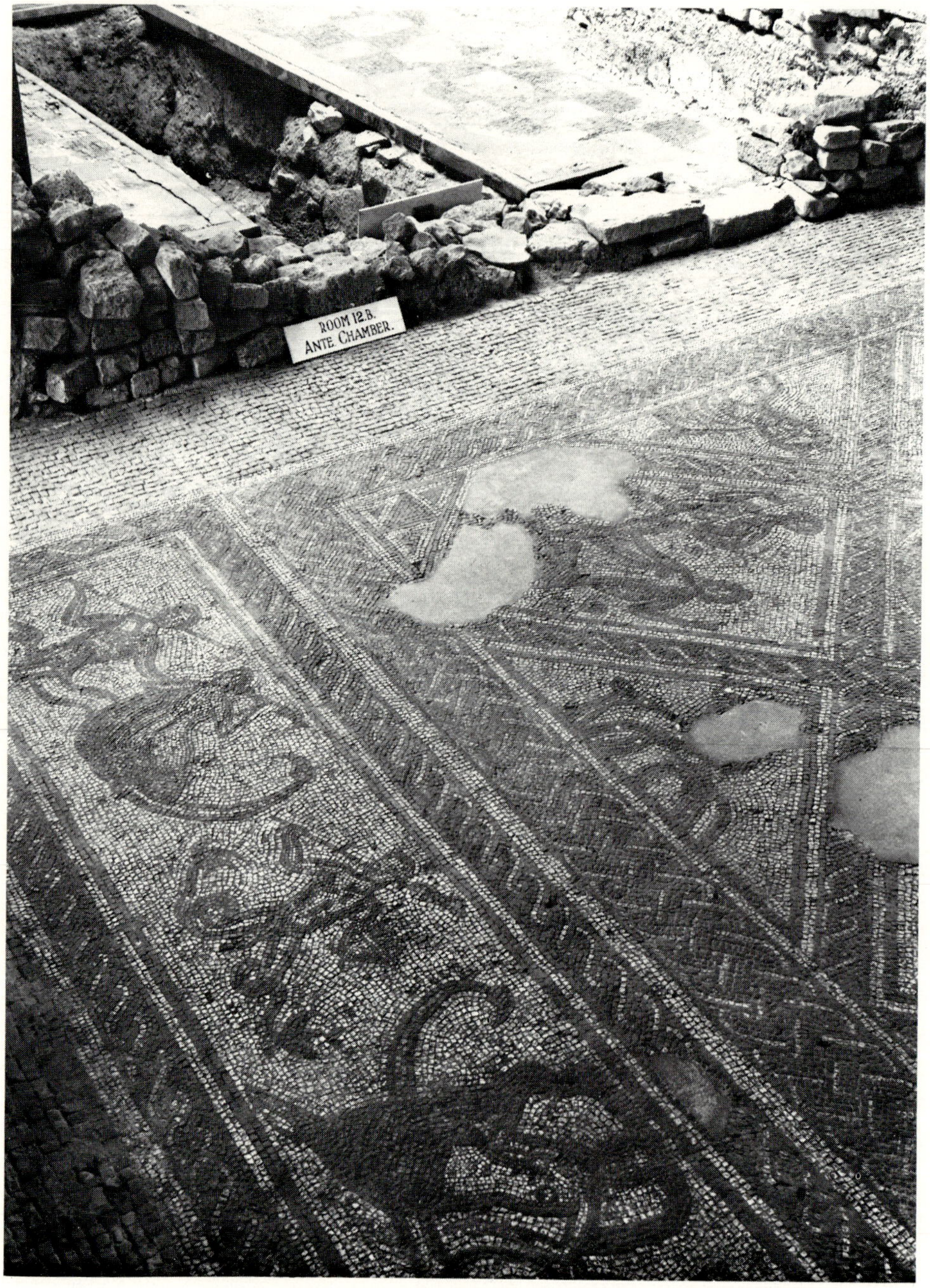
ROOM 12.B.
ANTE. CHAMBER.

85 B.C. Like all Celtic peoples, they were governed by the Druids, with a powerful priestly caste of religious leaders. The Druids on the Isle of Wight worshipped Hu Gudarn as a supreme deity but also offered allegiance to the goddess Alwen, the Celtic counterpart of Venus.

Wherever the Druids settled, they revered the oak, and the Isle of Wight was no exception. Three places were held to be exceptionally sacred. The main oak was Hexel, also known as Gabhanodorum, which is now covered by the quiet waters of Bembridge Harbor. Small sailing craft now skim across the waters where the supreme leader of the Druids, the Arch-Druid, once lived. Another sacred place was the pinnacle of Ur, now known as Needle Rock. The third grove was the Long Stone of Mottistone, a fine erect pillar of iron sandstone that is the oldest example of man's handiwork on the island.

Wight is famous for its glorious sunsets—sunsets reminiscent of the distant past when the Arch-Druid poised motionless over a human sacrifice in one of the sacred groves. As the red sun sent its last scarlet rays, the sacrifice was accomplished, symbolizing not death but the power and mystery of new birth. By such sacrifices, the Druids believed that the dying sun was able to sustain itself, just as the blood sacrifice gave strength to the living. These strange rites were part of the secrets of man's magic and cunning arts.

When the Druids ruled the island, the human race was young and just emerging from savagery. But then came the Romans, the Saxons, the Danes, and the Roman soldiery. Whereas the Druids had used their wisdom to lighten the dark work of savagery, the others came to conquer and despoil the land. Wight was conquered by the Roman general Vespasian in A.D. 43. There are several well-preserved examples of Roman architecture on the island, the most famous of which is the tesselated pavement of a large Roman villa in the little village of Brading.

This Roman mosaic pavement, depicting astrological signs, dates back to the time of the Roman invasion of the Isle of Wight.

At this time, the island was inhabited by the Jutes, a race of German origin who ultimately became known as the Anglo-Saxons. In the fifth century, they settled in Kent, Southampton, and the adjacent New Forest on the mainland, but their influence lingered on in the Isle of Wight. In the eleventh century, the Danes used the island as a base from which they could raid the English coast. With its serene atmosphere, gracious scenery, and health-giving waters, the Isle of Wight was an ideal place for war-weary troops.

With the Norman invasion of England in 1066, Wight settled down to a remarkable stable life, a prelude to a strong Christian administration. As always when the Romans and Normans invaded, the main Druidic forces moved to other islands, but the close proximity of Stonehenge seems to indicate that they continued to use the island for specific seasonal festivals.

The aura of spirituality has always been strong in Wight. Many religious groups made it their headquarters, including a dedicated number of Benedictine monks who built Quarr Abbey. The island has always been a haven for those seeking creative inspiration as well. The English poet John Keats was a resident of Shanklin. Sir Alfred Tennyson, poet laureate to Queen Victoria, made his home on the island and found inspiration there for many of his famous poems. But it fell to an American poet, Henry Wadsworth Longfellow, to capture the serenity of the island in a poem, a stanza of which is carved on a stone for all to see. Generation after generation of travelers have rested their weary feet on the soft downlands of Wight; others have drunk the magical health-giving waters seeping from natural springs or harnessed to wells. The Isle of Wight is an experience in nostalgia, stemming from the Druids, Roman legions, Anglo-Saxons, Benedictine monks, Christian ministers, and creative artistic spirits. It is a place well equipped to rejuvenate the mind, body, and spirit of all who visit there.

This Roman bath is part of a villa that was built in the little village of Brading.

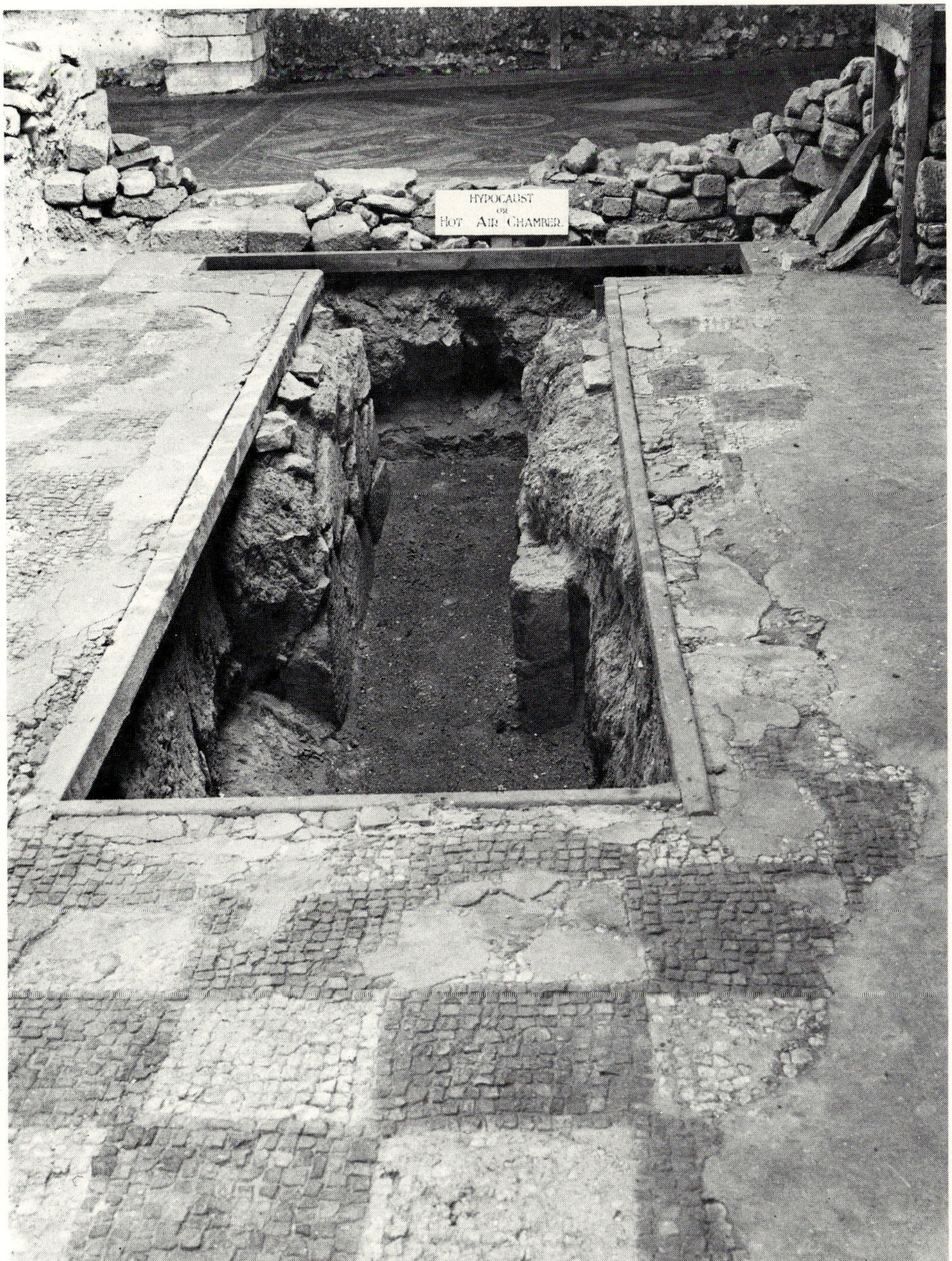
HYPOCAUST
OR
HOT AIR CHAMBER.

> O Traveller, stay thy weary feet;
> Drink of this fountain pure and sweet;
> It flows for rich and poor the same.
> Then go thy way, remembering still
> The wayside well beneath the hill,
> The cup of water in His name.
>
> *Longfellow*

The old churches of the island are beautiful examples of architectural splendor spanning the centuries. They include one dedicated to Saint Blasius, founded in the sixteenth century at the foot of Shanklin Down, and another dedicated to Saint Boniface, built on the site of an earlier Anglo-Saxon church in Bonchurch. Monks from the Abbey of Lyra, in Normandy, built the church at Bonchurch, and although they were Normans, they dedicated it to a Saxon saint. Saint Boniface was a Devonshire monk who came to the island in the eighth century and stayed to preach the Christian religion to a community of fishermen. A wooden cross on the high cliff, called Pulpit Rock, is said to have been the favorite place for the saint to talk to his flock. Saint Boniface left the island to go on a missionary expedition to Germany, where he died a martyr's death in 755. Saint Boniface Church is the most complete Norman church on the island today. In the churchyard lie the remains of one of the most renowned but controversial of all Victorian poets, Algernon Charles Swinburne. Lord Macaulay and Charles Dickens often visited Bonchurch and left something of their own creative genius implanted in the atmosphere.

Godshill Church was built on a site originally known as "The Devil's Acre." A local legend tells the story that when the church was being built, it was constantly demolished by supernatural means originating from the Devil himself. But angels came to help rebuild the church, so good overcame evil; the Devil gave up his mischievous antics and admitted defeat, and the church was finally built. There is a history of Druidic witchcraft on the island, but it is associated with the practice of white magic and healing. The Devil's Acre is the only area tainted by association with the one-time Prince of Light, the fallen angel who became the adversary of God himself.

American poet Henry Wadsworth Longfellow knew the serenity of the Isle of Wight
and commemorated its healing water and wells in this poem.

(Above) In the churchyard of Saint Boniface Church lie the remains of the renowned Victorian poet Algernon Charles Swinburne. (Right) This arch stands as a gateway to history, leading to historic Carisbrooke Castle, where King Charles I was imprisoned in 1647.

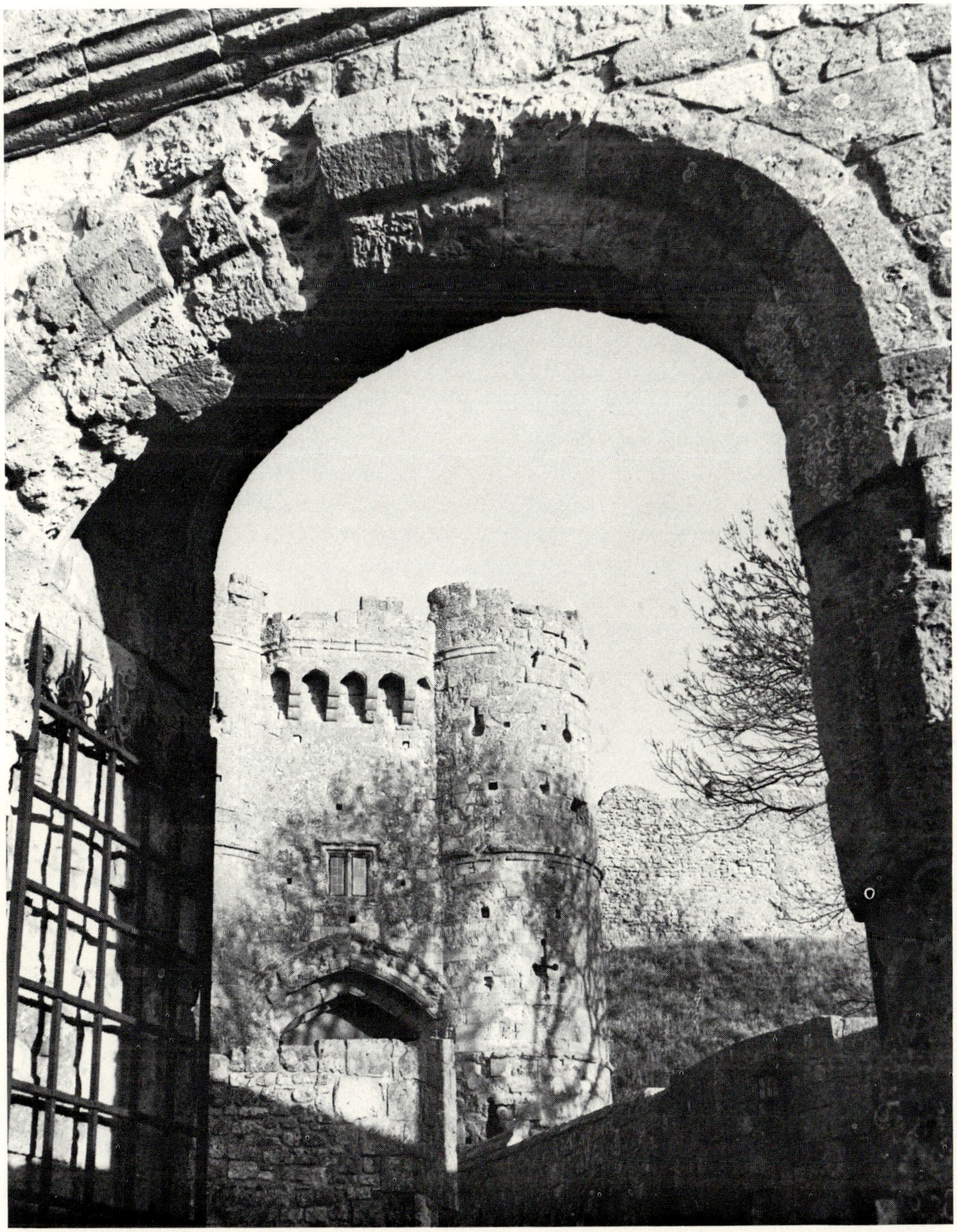

Historic Carisbrooke Castle stands on a naturally strategic point of high ground dominating the town of Newport, the only town on the island without its own coastline. Although the Normans built the castle at Carisbrooke, there is evidence to prove that the Romans saw the site's importance as a fortified camp long before the Normans set foot on the island. King Charles I was imprisoned in the castle in 1647, and his daughter, Elizabeth, is buried in the ancient Newport cemetery. Today, the castle is a partial ruin, but the remaining towers and archway stand as a memory of a fine substantial fortress.

The famous *Doomsday Book*, in which William I had land surveys recorded for tax purposes, contains many references to the small towns on the Isle of Wight, but we do not need to pore over this ancient document to know that the island is of great antiquity. Even in the silent serenity of any of the remote pathways, anyone with a modicum of psychic awareness can feel the presence of the past invading the present. For beautiful though the island is, it is human beings who leave their imprint on the atmosphere. Dr. Herbert Read sums it all up in his *Education Through the Arts:* "The individual's touch of color contributes, however imperceptibly, to the beauty of the landscape, his note is a necessary, though unnoticed, element in the universal harmony." On the Isle of Wight, human consciousness blends with the cosmos to make a visit there a remarkable psychic experience.

# *Eighteen*

## The Channel Isles

This group of islands consists of Jersey, Guernsey, Alderney, Sark, and Herm. Like the Isle of Wight, these islands are situated in the shipping lanes of the English Channel, making them within easy reach of the mainland of England and France.

The earliest inhabitants of the islands were of Celtic origin, followed by the invasion forces of Romans, Saxons, and Jutes. During the early Celtic period, the Druids were in existence in England and in Brittany, France. The Channel Isles are redolent with legends of both Breton and English Druids, and there is abundant proof of their influence on the islands provided by the standing megalithic monuments, cromlechs, kistvaens, and menhirs. Despite this, the original ethnology and pre-Christian history of the islands have always been a matter of conjecture among scholarly historians, fostering many learned debates as to the influence of the Druidic Celts in this part of the world.

Christianity was introduced to the islands in about the fifth century. In the sixth century, Guernsey was visited by Saint Sampson of Dol, who gave his name to a small town and harbor on the island. Saint Marcou and Saint Magloire, missionaries of the same period, founded monasteries on Jersey and Sark. Another evangelist of this time was Saint Helerius, who gave his name to the most important town on Jersey, the popular resort city of St. Helier.

(Above) Mont Orgueil houses the crypt of Saint George, famous for his adventures in slaying the dragon. (Right) Le Hocar, an ancient martello tower, guards the coast from invasion.

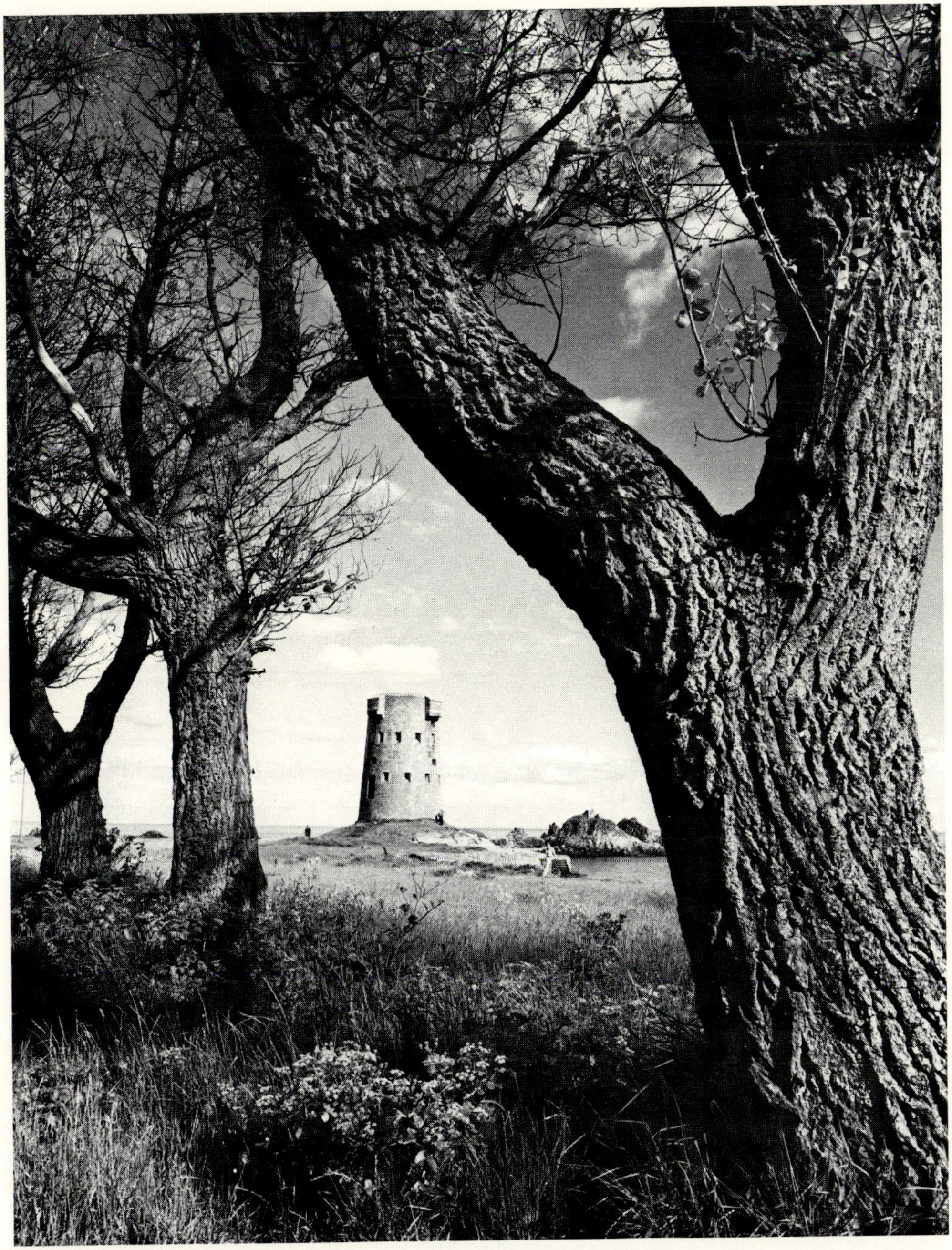

The islands were taken over by the Duke of Normandy in 933, but after the Norman invasion of England in 1066, the islanders were constantly shifting their allegiance from France to Britain and back again to France. This period was one in which the islands were enriched by fine ecclesiastic buildings with the typical Norman arches, but there was also a great deal of ruthlessness as religion became more and more linked with the political intrigues of both England and France. Henry V of England confiscated all priories on the islands that had maintained contact with Normandy. During the reign of Henry VI, a force was sent out to capture Mont Orgueil, famous for its crypt containing the bones of Saint George of dragon-slaying fame. The religious establishments were dissolved again in the reign of Henry VIII, and the Reformation was accepted almost cheerfully by the islanders who were beginning to get tired of being buffer states in a game of political chess. After the Reformation, the liturgy was translated into French, since the islanders spoke mainly French although now under British rule.

When Elizabeth I was on the throne, the Roman Catholics were persecuted; when she finally sanctioned the Presbyterian form of church government, the islands were flooded with Protestants from France. More periods of religious torment were in store for the islands, however, during the reign of James I. His struggle with Parliament stretched out to the islands, finding its roots for discontent in the diverse religions on the islands. Guernsey was fiercely Presbyterian and pro-Parliament, while Jersey adhered to Roman Catholicism and the royalist cause. There was not as much religious dissention on the less-inhabited islands of Alderney and Sark, and to this day, remnants of the Druidic cult and Wicca still hold sway. Remote and lonely Herm, whose main population was goats and birds, suffered less than the other islands.

Religion has always played a great part in the everyday life of the islanders, and wherever one goes, one comes across place names associated with numerous saints. For instance, eight of the ten parishes of Jersey bear the names of saints: Helier, Brelade, Clement John, Laurence Martin, Mary, Ouen,

Pierce Pesces and Passe Percee on the lonely island of Herm.

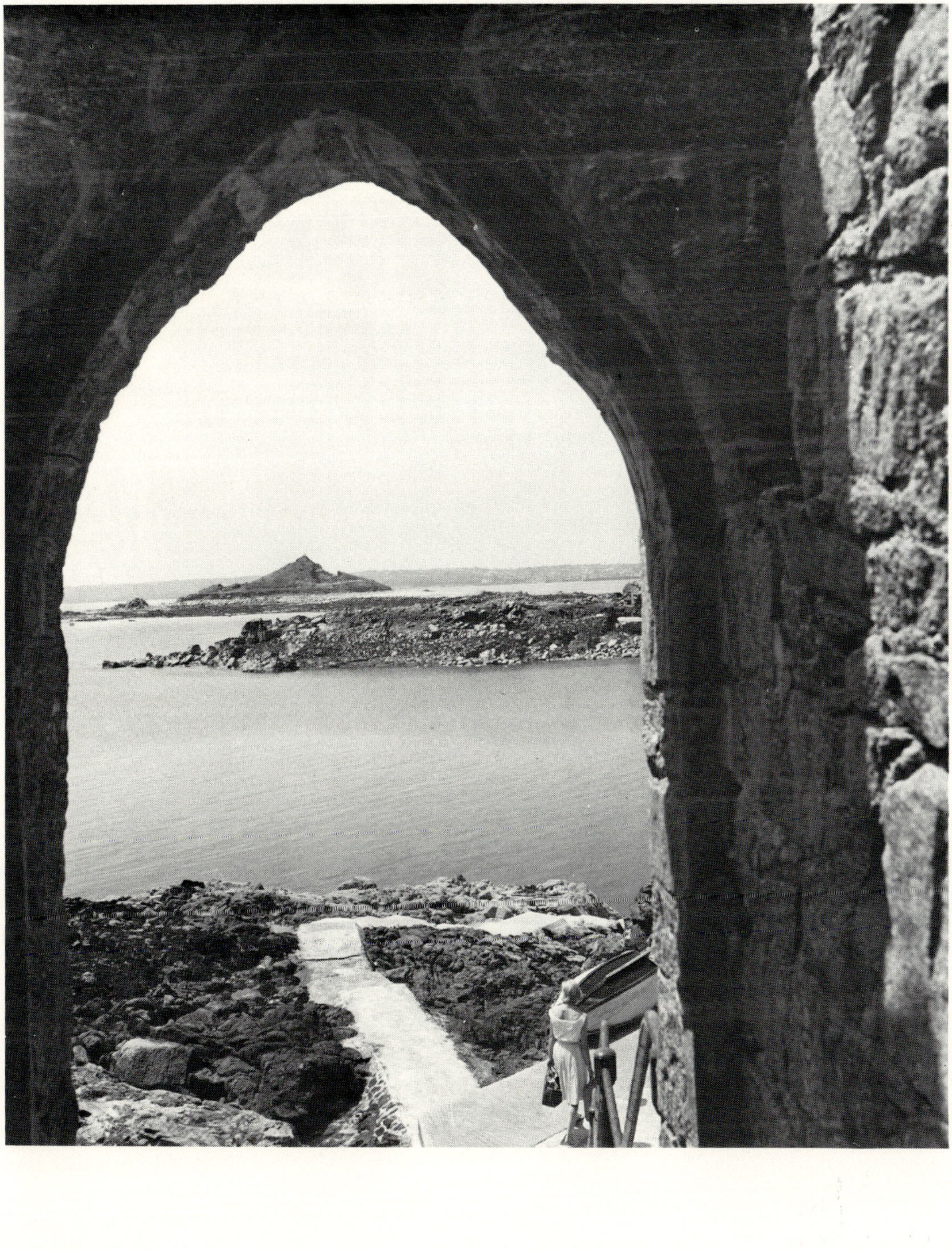

The Dolmen de la Hougar most probably served as a burial ground for Druidic priests.

The "Witches' Stones" on the Hermitage of Elizabeth Castle could have provided a restful moment for tired witches flying to a coven meeting.

Peter, and Saviour, the remaining two parishes being called Crouville and Trinity. Saint Brelade Church is probably one of the oldest on the island, dating from the twelfth century, but there are many chapels of an earlier date, including the Chapel of the Fisherman at St. Brelade and the picturesque one located on the grounds of the manor of Rozel.

Also on Jersey is the castle of Mont Orgueil, of which there are considerable remains. The castle was founded on the site of a former Roman stronghold, and one part of it is still called "Caesar's Fort." A fine example of a cromlech stands near Mont Orgueil. There is also a fine example of a dolmen called The Hougar, and it is likely that this was a burial ground for Druidic priests.

Like Jersey and the neighboring part of France, Guernsey retains many traces of early inhabitants in cromlechs and menhirs, of which the most notable is the cromlech at L'Ancresse, in the northern part of the island. If you want to buy a "Witches' Stone," you can still get one today from George Le Couteur. Now age seventy, George has spent his life working with Guernsey granite, from which all the finest Witches' Stones are made. These are flat slabs of stone jutting out from a chimney stack or gable end. The original idea was that such stones provided resting places for witches as they flew to their coven meetings at the time of the full moon; the jutting-out stones were sufficiently large for a tired witch to rest for a few moments before continuing her flight. In ancient times, no new building was put up on the islands without its own Witches' Stone; today, many of these stones can still be seen on the islands' older houses. Until World War II, there was a constant demand for such stones, but now the interest has dwindled to being a commodity for tourists.

When we reach the Channel Isles, the spiritual guardianship in the circle of magic islands around Great Britain seems to become weak. Since the psychic forces were dispersed from Stonehenge in England and Brittany in France, there was no need for the islands to become a complete retreat for the ancient pre-Christian religion. But the forces of Christianity left their own aura of sanctity on the islands despite the numerous religious and political disputes. All five islands are worth a visit, but few people will feel the same strong psychic vibrations that permeate the western group of islands.

# Nineteen

## Scilly: The Isles of the Blessed

If the Isle of Man seems reluctant to show its esoteric mysteries and magic to the people of the world, the Scilly Isles do not. Although there are some 140 tiny isles in the group, only 5 are inhabited: St. Mary's, Tresco, St. Martin's, St. Agnes, and Bryher. The Scilly Isles are like a group of courtesans opening their arms and willing to show their charms to all who care to stand and stare.

Only twenty-eight miles from the southwestern tip of England, these isles are like a dream come true, a paradise of flowers; warmed by the Gulf Stream, the Scillies defy winter. They present an image of halcyon days, with their deep turquoise sea, gleaming beaches, and neat spic-and-span rows of houses.

But the Scillies are also like the Lorelei, the sirens who called to sailors with their sweet songs—only to wreck their ships. The sea here is deceptively gentle, capable of changing to a thundering churn of white froth as if a giant were angry with the world. Many dangerous crosstides race among the rocky crags and islets. A person must be born and bred on these islands to understand the wayward whims of the sea and the wealth of history that lurks on the islands. Long ago, in the Bronze Age, men lived on many more of the islands that now look like desolate rocks in the sea, capable only of supporting bird life or seals whose voices mingle with the wind to provide a never-ending dirge.

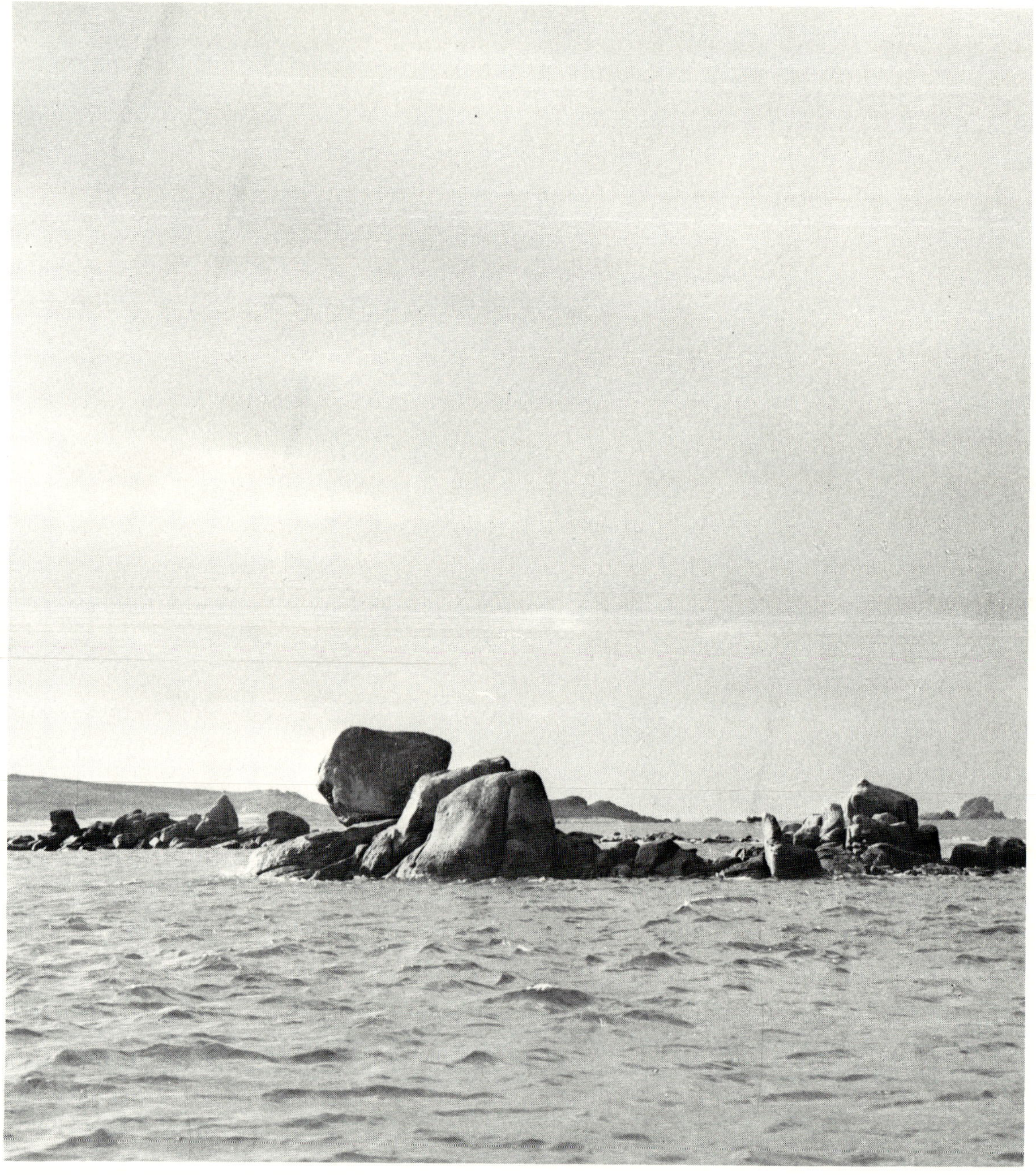

Once, according to legend, a country called Lyonnesse linked the Scillies with England, and on its now vanished soil, the various knights of King Arthur fought a grim battle against the troublesome rebellious Sir Mordred. It was Merlin, the mighty wizard, who chanted the magical words that made Lyonnesse sink into the jaws of the ocean. Sir Mordred and his rebel knights were drowned, but King Arthur and his noble band were safely entrenched on high ground, which is now called the Scilly Isles.

Today, other magicians live on the islands, coaxing flowers to bloom all through the winter, vying with Holland in the exquisite blooms they produce for the markets of the world. No one is quite sure who introduced daffodils to the island; time has obscured the identity. Perhaps it was a monk or a Dutch sea captain, but whoever it was brought a pot of gold to start off the economy of the islands.

The Scillies are all rocks and hills, a terrain that seems ill-fitting for the masses of softly blooming, glamorous spring flowers. As the sea defies man's ingenuity to cross it and conquer, so the flowers defy the harshness of the terrain, a continuation of the granite backbone of Cornwall.

Men have lived on these islands for over four thousand years, and there are some forty-five ancient burial chambers on the islands. One of the most famous of these, and certainly one which has been well excavated, is situated on Porth Hellick Down. Cremation was carried out by the ancients who lived and died on the Scillies, and some seventy burial urns have already been excavated. There is a theory that back in the Bronze Age, these islands were a burial place for distinguished dead. Here, dead chiefs and heroes could dream in their long sleep of immortality, with the sea singing a constant requiem. But there is probably another reason for the dead being buried on Scilly, and not all those ashes in the urns belonged to heroes. Some probably belonged to enemies of men on the mainland, who believed that departed spirits could not cross water; the turbulence of the seas added to this idea. Nevertheless, whoever decided that Scilly was to be a burial ground made sure that the dead were honorably and carefully placed in their last resting place. The burial chambers of Porth Hellick

The Scillies sweetly beckon to passing seafarers, but crossing between the islands claims many shipwreck victims.

Merlin, the mighty wizard, found sanctuary in the Scilly Isles.

Legend has it that these islands were formed when Merlin caused a country called Lyonnesse to sink into the ocean.

150

Down are a natural fortification of huge rocks and massive stones that could be safely dragged into position to close up the entrances.

Roman coins have been found on the island dating back to A.D. 69–375, more than a thousand years after the Bronze Age and four hundred years before the Iron Age. Before the Romans came, those intrepid ocean travelers, the Phoenicians, came to trade for tin. On the beach at Nornour, over three hundred brooches were found; these were certainly not for local trading, but were more likely part of a store kept for trading with the Phoenicians.

Before spring flowers made the Scillies into a modern garden of paradise, the islands thrived on trading jewelry and later on a highly organized business of smuggling. Even the sea contributed to the industry of the island, for the burning of kelp, a type of seaweed, produced soda ash. These islands were well named the Islands of the Blessed, but their second name is the Fortunate Isles, and fortunate indeed were the merchants who did their trading here. Even the puppy-faced seals gambolling on the rocks once made their sad contribution to trade when a man's business status was estimated by his ability to sport a full-length sealskin coat.

The Isle of Tresco contains a profusion of beauty from the ruins of Tresco Abbey, a couple of ruined castles, and the fabulous Abbey Gardens. Here, exotic plants not indigenous to the area grow in man-contrived precision, brought by sailors who knew that the owner of the island loved unusual plants. The gardens are like a subtropical forest, and it is hard to realize that man created them in the same latitude as frigid Newfoundland. No one knows if it is only the Gulf Stream that makes such beautiful plants thrive. Perhaps there is some of the old magic of Merlin around after all.

Passing through an arch of the medieval abbey, one is suddenly astounded to find row after row of regal figureheads staring with sightless eyes at the garden. Even more difficult to realize is that these figureheads once graced the prows of stately ships until they were wrecked by the deceptive waters of the pounding ocean. In the days when great sails proudly worked their way through the oceans of the world, these Blessed Islands were their death trap.

Of the numerous ancient burial chambers on the islands, those at Porth Hellick Down are among the most famous.

152

(Left) Massive stones comprise this entrance to a burial chamber at Porth Hellick Down. (Above) This burial chamber, of which the interior is shown here, is some four thousand years old.

(Above) It is hard to realize that these lush, exotic gardens of Tresco Abbey were created in the same latitude as frigid Newfoundland. (Right) These gracefully carved figureheads in Tresco Abbey are all that remain of ships wrecked in the dangerous waters around the Scilly Isles.

155

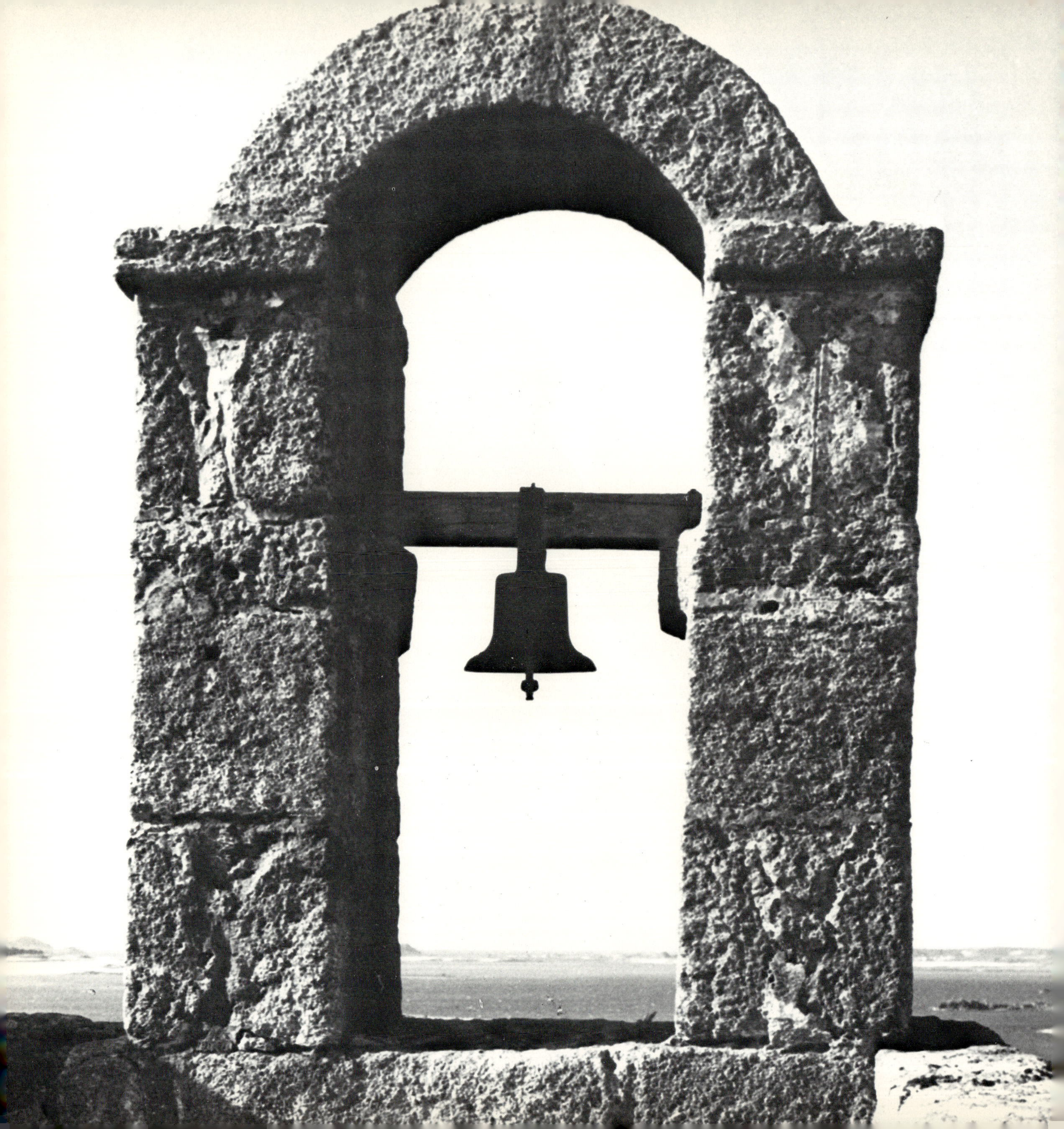

Star Castle was built as an outpost against the Spanish a few years after the Armada sailed by; today, its bell hangs in silence.

The owner of Tresco, Augustus Smith, gave this resting place of proud ships' figureheads the name of Valhalla—the hall of the slain, the name given by the Norsemen to the abode of the souls of those who had fallen in battle. It is easy to see how appropriate the name is.

Not all the ships came to a legitimate end by the vagaries of the ocean. Again something of the old magic of Merlin raises its head as we realize that the Scilly Isles housed men who thrived on deliberately wrecking ships and then plundering them. Until the late eighteenth century, a prayer was offered regularly at the Church of Saint Mary:

*We pray thee, O Lord, not that wrecks should happen, but if any wreck should happen, Thou wilt guide them into the Scilly Isles for the benefit of the poor inhabitants.*

With the ocean as an ally, there was little need for the prayer, and ships continued to be wrecked, bringing benefits to the inhabitants.

At the top of a hill in Hugh Town stands Star Castle, built by Sir Francis Godolphin as an outpost against the Spanish a few years after the Armada sailed by. Out at sea, Bishop Rock Light stands like a grim sentinel, flashing its lights as a warning to sailors. The Atlantic Ocean pounds away at the rock on which the graceful lighthouse is built, and there is nothing between this lighthouse and America.

The Scilly Isles have had a strange religious history since they were used as ceremonial burial grounds in the Bronze Age. Christian churches appeared on the island in the first century, but King Henry I gave all the churches and their lands to the Abbot and Church of Tavistock on the mainland. The monks remaining on the islands were allowed to share the spoils of ships wrecked at sea, but it is likely that the Scillian monks kept more than their legal half. In 1345, the Bishop of Exeter substituted secular priests for the regulars under the guardianship of the Abbot of Tavistock. The time was ripe for rebellion by the

At Shovel Rock, the indestructible stone and man-made anchor blend to express the spirit of the Scilly Isles. The sea is the protective guardian of these islands and the enemy of those who do not come with peace in their hearts to the Isles of the Blessed.

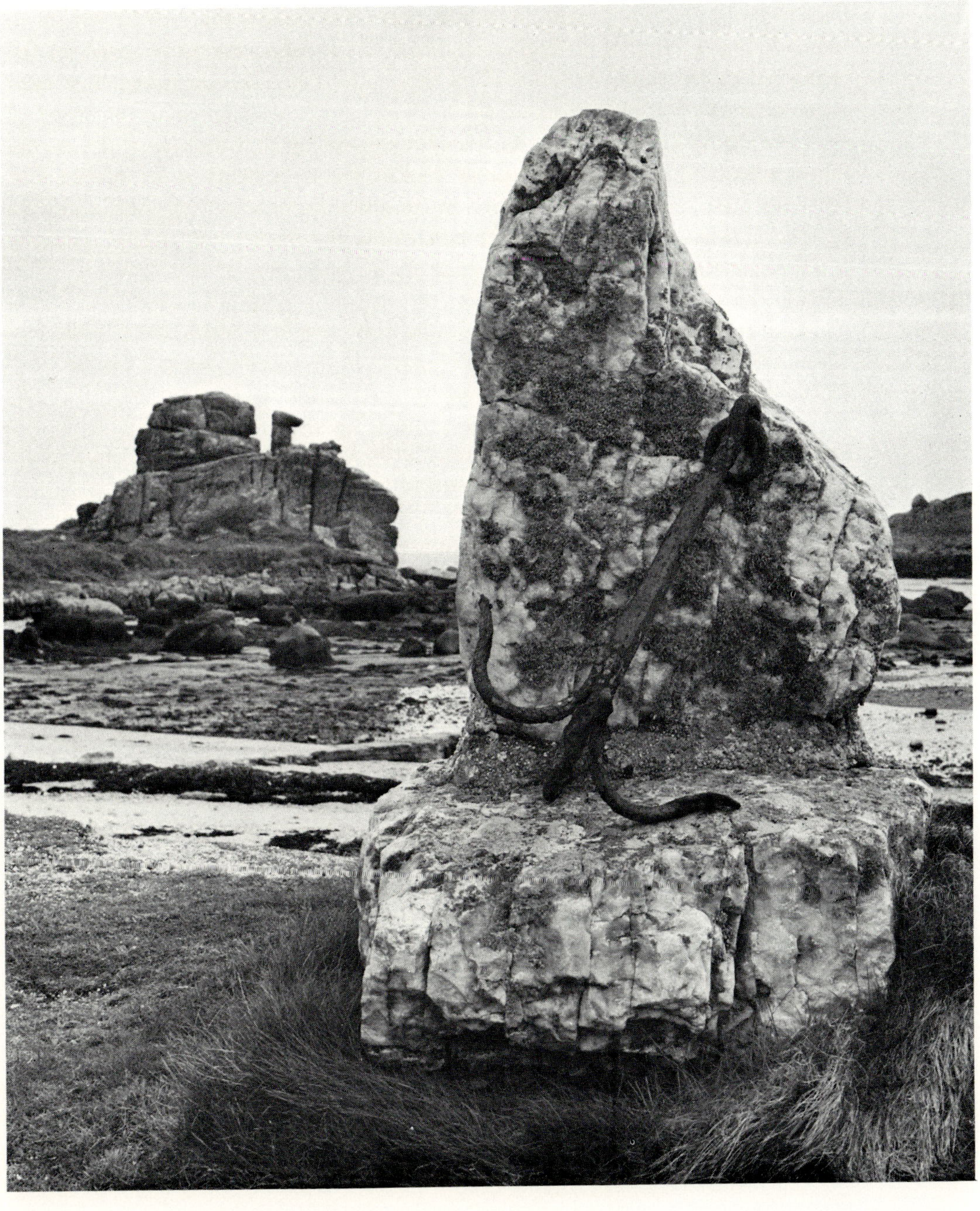

lordly families in Scilly, especially when the jurisdiction of the courts was given to the enemies of the Blanchminster family at the beginning of the fourteenth century. In 1345, the family petitioned the king to intervene against the constant encroachment on their lands by soldiers and the head of mainland monasteries. In 1547, Silvester Danvers, representing the Blanchminsters as coheir to the lands, sold out his share of the islands to Sir Thomas Seymour. When Seymour fell from his place as favorite to the monarch, the Scilly Isles fell into the hand of the Crown—not that there was much now for the Crown to take, since in suppressing the religious houses, it had already plundered much of the treasure kept in the churches. From this point onward, the wealth and influence of the churches fell to pieces, and all that remained was the memory of Merlin defying Lyonnesse and causing it to fall into the sea.

Whatever magic now remains on the islands belongs to Merlin, and it is of King Arthur and his knights that the visitor dreams as he walks on golden sands or through the fields of bright spring flowers. The magic of Merlin is as potent as the perfume of the flowers, and the memory of both brave and sinister deeds remains long after the visitor has left the islands.

The spirits in the burial chambers and the figureheads of ghostly ships mingle well in the Scilly Isles—the Isles of the Blessed, the Fortunate Islands—where fair flowers grow in places where no such flowers should ever bloom. The moaning voices of the puppy-faced seals mingle with the thunder of the sea, and above it all, Merlin laughs, knowing that the magic which men have within them is trapped when they see gold.